WHERE TOWN MEETS COUNTRY

WHERE TOWN MEETS COUNTRY

Problems of Peri-urban areas in Scotland

ROYAL SCOTTISH GEOGRAPHICAL SOCIETY SYMPOSIUM
MAY 1981

Edited on behalf of the Society by

A B CRUICKSHANK
University of Glasgow

ABERDEEN UNIVERSITY PRESS

First published 1982
Aberdeen University Press
A member of the Pergamon Group

British Library Cataloguing in Publication Data
Where town meets country
1. Suburbs—Scotland—Congresses
I. Cruickshank, A. B. II. Royal Scottish
Geographical Society
307.7′4   HT164.S/

ISBN 0-08-028442-6
ISBN 0-08-028443-4 Pbk

PRINTED IN GREAT BRITAIN
THE UNIVERSITY PRESS
ABERDEEN

CONTENTS

FIGURES

TABLES

ACKNOWLEDGEMENTS

The editor wishes to thank all the individuals and organisations represented in this volume for agreeing so readily to take part in the Symposium, for having their manuscripts available to meet the deadline for publication and for providing accompanying illustrative material. The Forestry Commission and the Countryside Commission for Scotland kindly provided exhibitions at the Symposium. He would also like to thank Professor V.B. Proudfoot, St. Andrews University and Professor M.F. Thomas, Stirling University, members of the RSGS, Symposium Sub-Committee, Mr.D.G. Moir, Secretary of the RSGS and Professor I.B. Thomson, Glasgow University, for help and support during the preparations for the Symposium.

Miss M. Coyle and Miss B. Fraser undertook the secretarial work for the editor and the manuscript was typed by Mrs. I. Mack.

The editor and publishers also thank the following for permission to publish copyright material.

Department of Agriculture and Fisheries for Scotland	Fig. 7.1.
Forestry Commission	Fig. 6.1
Scottish Development Department	Fig. 7.2
Scottish Development Agency	Fig. 5.1, 5.2 & 5.3
Edinburgh University Press	Fig. 6.2
Association of American Geographers & J.T. Pierce	Fig. 1.1
Strathclyde Regional Council	Regional Key Diagram

The illustration used for Figure 6.2 is of Sir Henry Steuart's planting machine of the early 19th century. It has been used recently by Mr. A.A. Tait to illustrate his book 'The Landscape Garden in Scotland 1735-1835'. His publishers, the Edinburgh University Press, have kindly supplied the plate for reproduction.

PREFACE

This volume of papers and discussion arises out of a symposium organised by the editor on behalf of the Royal Scottish Geographical Society and held in the University of Glasgow on 29th May 1981. The theme of Peri-Urban Areas, or as these areas are more commonly called in Scotland Countryside around Towns, was chosen in order to focus attention on the wide range of problems and possibilities currently being encountered by land owners, land users and planners operating in such areas. This is the zone where Town meets Country and where rural interests and urban interests overlap, sometimes resulting in conflict. Although this volume largely has Scotland as the areal focus of its concern, there is a clear intention that the philosophies and methodologies herein explored should be of much wider interest and application.

In inviting contributions, the Editor was aware of many organisations having interests in these areas and of differences of policies and priorities but that time and space were not available to allow presentation and publication of papers representative of all viewpoints. However, a major aim of the Symposium was to bring together, from many disparate backgrounds, experts and lay persons sharing a common concern with peri-urban areas and by so doing to stimulate discussion and foster mutual recognition of the validity of the various approaches.

It is hoped that the publication of this volume will further these objectives.

CHAPTER 1
PERI-URBAN AREAS: A REVIEW

Alistair Cruickshank
University of Glasgow

ABSTRACT

This paper examines the proposals relating to peri-urban areas in the Strathclyde
Structure Plan, First Review and Alteration 1981, consultation draft, particularly
with regard to the constraints of agricultural land quality, Greenbelt policy and
environmental considerations on the selection of land for future development.
These proposals are set against a review of some recent publications relating to
peri-urban areas.

KEYWORDS

Peri-urban areas; Countryside around towns; Greenbelt; urban fringe management;
Structure Plan Review; Strathclyde.

The First Review and Alteration, Consultative Draft: Strathclyde Structure Plan
SRC (1981) was produced in March 1981. This First Review is in response to the
direction by the Secretary of State for Scotland requiring the Regional Council
to submit an Alteration to the Structure Plan which would, among other things,
re-assess housing supply and demand and undertake a comprehensive review of rural
matters covering general countryside strategy, settlement policy, landscape,
tourism and recreation, agriculture and forestry and nature conservation.

Both these issues focus attention on the peri-urban areas of Strathclyde and it is
the intention of this paper to examine the proposals set out in this Consultative
Draft against the background of a more general review of recent contributions to
the study of peri-urban areas.

In this volume Pead (Chapter 12) examines the problems of his regional planning
authority in managing the land supply for development, the demand for such land
being concentrated in the peri-urban areas, and requiring the release of greenfield sites. Among eight constraints to be evaluated in identifying these sites
are:-

(2) agricultural land quality
(7) the effects of the approved Greenbelt policy and
(8) a series of environmental constraints   (SRC 1981a)

1

Each of these is worthy of further consideration.

Agricultural land quality

The statement that, 'Country planners need not be too much concerned, it would
seem, about the selection of land for non agricultural uses.', A.E.I.R.O. (1944)
may represent the first salvo in a protracted debate which has continued ever
since, largely from entrenched positions and with varying degrees of intensity.
The issue has largely been the amount of agricultural land lost annually to urban
and associated development and the resultant consequences following from such
losses. Some of the more recent contributions to the debate have been, in the U.K.
Best (1976a) Best (1976b) Merchant (1976) Wibberley(1976) Best (1977) Coleman
(1977) Allison (1978) Gilg (1978) Rogers (1978) Blacksell (1979) S.D.D. (1980)
Elson (1981a) Hebbert (1981) Moss (1981) Wibberley (1981), in Europe, O.E.C.D.
(1976) Best (1979), in the U.S.A., Hart (1976) Vining, Bieri & Strauss (1977)
Platt (1981) and Canada, Manning & McCuaig (1977) Pierce (1979). It is generally
conceded that some loss of agricultural land is inevitable and more recently the
argument has tended to focus on the loss of prime agricultural land. 'Urbanisat-
ion usually affects farm land of the best quality' OECD (1979) because, 'histori-
cally urban growth has tended to favour those sites possessing better-quality
agricultural land', Pierce (1981) as figure 1.1 demonstrates for Canada.

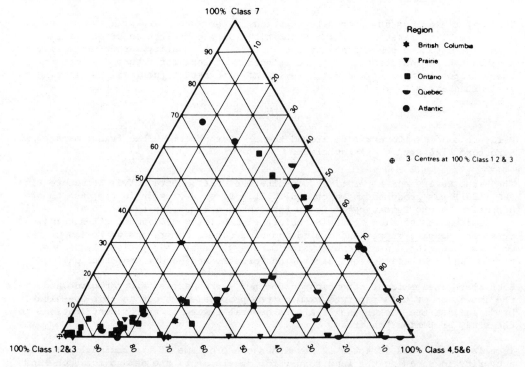

Fig. 1.1 CONVERSION OF RURAL LAND TO URBAN: CANADA
Reproduced by permission from *The Professional Geographer* of the Association of American Geographers,
Vol 33,   2, May 1981, p. 169, figure 3, J. T. Pierce.

In view of continuing government policy against the use of prime agricultural land
for development, DAFS (Chapter 7) the scale of loss of such land in Scotland must
give cause for concern. The Strathclyde Review, SRC (1981b) suggests that an

explanation may lie in the fact that most losses of prime agricultural land have
been in parcels of less than 5 ha, i.e. below the current threshold of referral to
the Secretary of State. In England the threshold was reduced from 10 acres to 5
acres in 1976, and it is understood that a similar threshold is currently being
considered for Scotland. However the Strathclyde Review proposes a general
presumption against development on prime agricultural land.

Diamond (1979), perhaps tongue in cheek, makes an interesting presumption that the
National Planning Guidelines for Scotland implied that permission for development
on land of quality below B plus would not involve the Scottish Development Department. It is to be hoped that today no such single criterion would be the signal for
disinterest particularly so in the case of usage of the Land Capability Classification, which should never be employed without qualification. This classification
operates essentially on the basis of, the fewer the physical constraints on the
agricultural use of a parcel of land, the higher the grade awarded. Thus soils
ideally suited to one highly profitable agricultural use may be classified as low
grade because of physical restraints on its use for other agricultural purposes.
Further, the loss of an area of prime land in a location isolated from the remainder of a holding may be much less significant to the viable operation of that
holding than the loss of an equivalent area of land of a lower grade which is an
integral part of the holding. As Ken MacDonald (Chapter 4) illustrates there is
a need for positive action to remedy agricultural ills on the urban fringe. There
is a need to identify the characteristics of individual land holdings in peri-
urban areas and to establish their current economic and environmental potential
as a prerequisite of remedial action.

Are there grounds for establishing that certain sectors of the urban fringe should
be designated less favoured areas so attracting higher levels of grant under the
Agriculture and Horticulture Grant Scheme of 1980? Munton (1981) established a
land classification according to land maintenance categories approximately as
follows:-

    I Land in good heart appropriately farmed

    II Land displaying evidence of mis-management

    III Derelict and semi-derelict land

which when applied by him to the London Green Belt produced the data shown in
Table 1.1 below

Table 1.1 Proportion of land area in each category.

	I	II	III
All land	64.7	29.8	5.5
Land let on short term	24.3	50.7	25.0
Land adjacent to residential areas	34.0	46.7	19.3
Hobby Farms	41.8	51.3	7.0
Horsi-culture	47.4	40.9	11.7

To what extent should these figures be taken as an indication that Hobby farms and
Horsi-culture are suitable land uses for the most difficult areas of the urban
fringe? Alternatively to what extent do these types of land use occupy stable

areas of the urban fringe which in the hands of a commercial farmer would display
an even higher proportion of the area in category I? Certainly, suitable landscaped areas used for these purposes and public open space established as a by-
product of planted amenity woodlands can be most sympathetically developed as
residential areas of high amenity. The agricultural land quality is largely
irrelevant to such uses, however when the full results of the survey are made
available it will be interesting to note where and under what conditions there
are strong and weak correlations between category I land and prime agricultural
land.

Green Belt Policy

The papers by Alan Aitken (Chapter 11) and Andrew Dawson (Chapter 10) which
discuss aspects of the past operation of the Clydeside and Edinburgh Green Belts
appear to confirm that these have operated as effective controls on development.
In England and Wales it has been argued, Elson (1979, 1981b) that the establishment
of Green Belts has been justified on the basis of their being all purpose policies
and an alternative to the creation and operation of a, 'complicated priority zoning
scheme for agricultural protection and selective recreational provisions'. Evidence
suggests that the clear identification of their extent and the psychological impact
of the name have heightened the degree of acceptance of Green Belts as agricultural
preserves. However, this is not to say that no development has taken place in
Green Belts. In a study of the West Midlands Conurbation, JURUE (1977) the authors
note with some surprise the very high level of applications for development within
the Green Belt in the period 1968 to 1973 despite a clear awareness by the applicants
of the planning authorities' stated Green Belt policies. It is suggested that the
potentially high value of a planning permission in the Green Belt may have been an
incentive although the record of success of applications was very low. Perhaps it
is more relevant to present policy proposals to note that in 1968-69 3.5 ha. or 1%
of the Green Belt land applied for was released but an acceleration in percentage
released is evident over the period culminating in 32.9 ha. or approximately 14%
land release in 1972-73 indicating increasing uncertainty in the operation of a
policy which would of itself stimulate further pressure through increased numbers
of applications. Thus while Brian Parnell is in tune with current government
thinking in urging a flexibility of approach to land use change within a continuum
of countryside around towns from the urban fringe outwards it appears unlikely that
his suggestion that the term, 'green belt' be dropped, will find acceptance in the
near future. Although Brian Parnell sees the prospect of loss of agricultural
land in the urban fringe being compensated for by greater security for farmers on
the land remaining if the flexible approach is adopted, 'countryside interests
and pressure groups have sought to obtain clear, defensible urban boundaries,
partly to enable farmers to use the full potential range of husbandry practices
and also to seek a reduction in planning blight or uncertainty so that open land
may secure reasonable investment. Elson (1981b).

Whatever the mechanisms adopted it appears that uncertainty must be minimised. The
OECD Council includes among its recommendations to member countries that:

'When regional or local land use plans prove necessary, these should provide for
zones reserved for agriculture, either specifically or in conjunction with other
compatible uses such as ecological reserves or recreation, and these agricultural
zones should be assured of a reasonably long duration and be subject to revision
before term only for imperative reasons and in accordance with the recognised
zoning procedures' OECD (1979).

Uncertainty can take many forms for farmers on the urban fringe Thompson (1977)
Coppock (1977) and as Sandy Ross (Chapter 8) notes these can impose many types of
penalties upon farmers.   John Mackay (Chapter 3) mentions the mental and

emotional stress upon farmers brought on through worry of what <u>may</u> happen because
of trespass or other actions by the public. Uncertainty may also be extended to
encompass the financial pressures upon landowners to sell land, to realise 'hope
value' as the differential between current use value and value zones for development assumes astronomical proportions OECD (1979), Morris (1977). This is the rock
upon which so many zoning policies have foundered and most authorities would
consider that this will continue to be the case unless the differential in value
of similar types of land brought about solely by being zoned differently is compensated for.

Various attempts to do this have been made,ranging from differential taxation
(Lapping 1975, Gardner et al 1977) rewarding those who continue active cultivation
in <u>pressured rural areas,</u> (which as identified by Elson (1981b p.49) are those
areas of countryside, 'deformed by the presence of all pervasive urban-generated
development pressures') to direct Governmental intervention in the development
land market as in the U.K. through the Community Land Act 1975 (Lievesley 1976).
The latter was designed to operate in tandem with Structure and Local Plans and
its repeal in 1980 leaves a situation of imbalance which,momentarily coinciding
with an economic depression has,to date,not been fully exposed. However, economic
recovery accompanied by renewed pressures for the conversion of agricultural land
particularly if accompanied by continuing agricultural depression could have
seriously disruptive consequences in peri-urban areas.

It may be that the Green Belt designation can do much to maintain order on the
urban fringe but one resultant may be that development is diverted into the countryside beyond the Green Belt, the so-called 'leap frogging' phenomenon Davidson &
Wibberley (1977), Hovinen (1977). Is a rural settlement policy sufficient to
successfully restrain such development? Elson (1981a). Past evidence would suggest
that the answer must be, 'No', if such a policy is not part of a wider and co-ordinated strategy.

Today population concentrations are characterised by polynuclear patterns of settlement having interlocking daily urban systems and a shared enveloping countryside,
the latter serving as a reserve of development land and the locus of recreation for
the urban population. The evolution of these complex systems has been paralleled
by the development of a series of planning measures applied on an areal basis in the
U.K. peri-urban areas. The first of these were the Green Belts to be followed albeit
in a piecemeal fashion by a series of measures to meet particular requirements, such
as National Parks, (in England & Wales), National Nature Reserves, Areas of out-
standing natural beauty and Sites of Special Scientific Interest. The preparation
of Structure Plans consequent upon the reorganisation of Local Government has
afforded the opportunity to reassess some of these measures and to bring all within
a co-ordinated framework. Thus in England and Wales, Green Belt redesignation can
be seen as a signficant test of two new approaches to countryside planning, which
can be distinguished: 'rural zonation' and 'multi-use and management' (Hebbert(1979).

This co-ordinated approach to countryside is prominent in the Strathclyde Structure
Plan Review. Broad zones are proposed encompassing the whole Region. The designation of an area as <u>Countryside Around Towns</u> SRC (1981) - the use of the term
Peri-urban Areas, a synonym, in international literature may be seen as an attempt
to surmount translation difficulties - is a new and significant departure. The
outer edge of this zone would not be rigidly defined but would merge into an outer
zone of <u>Remoter Rural Areas.</u> Fig. X.1 Regional Key Diagram illustrating this zonation
scheme is incorporated in this volume.

While they are not direct parallels there are certain correspondences between the
proposed Strathclyde zonation and zones identified by OECD (1979) and Gilg (1980)
and Elson (1981b) as demonstrated in Table 1.2 and Figure 1.2.

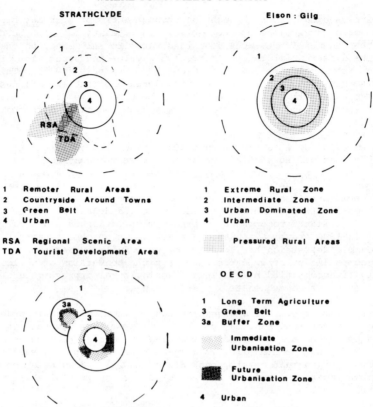

STRATHCLYDE

Elson : Gilg

1   Remoter Rural Areas
2   Countryside Around Towns
3   Green Belt
4   Urban

RSA   Regional Scenic Area
TDA   Tourist Development Area

1   Extreme Rural Zone
2   Intermediate Zone
3   Urban Dominated Zone
4   Urban

▨   Pressured Rural Areas

O E C D

1   Long Term Agriculture
3   Green Belt
3a Buffer Zone

▨   Immediate
    Urbanisation Zone

■   Future
    Urbanisation Zone

4   Urban

Fig. 1.2   PLANNING ZONES

TABLE 1.2 Rural Land: planning zones

O.E.C.D. 1979	Elson (1981) & Gilg (1980)	Strathclyde Regional Council 1981
Long Term Agricultural Zones	Extreme Rural Zone Intermediate Zone.	Remote Rural Areas Countryside Around Towns
Zones which will be urbanized in time	Urban Dominated Zone Pressured Rural Areas (Part)	Certain Urban Fringe areas of Green Belt and Countryside around towns
Zones to be urbanized immediately	Urban Dominated Zone Pressured Rural Areas (Part)	
Green Belts & Buffer Zones	Urban Dominated Zone Pressured Rural Areas (Part)	Green Belt Countryside Around Towns
Buffer Zones of smaller size		Overlap areas e.g. Regional scenic Areas Tourist Development Areas

In Strathclyde the proposed approach of co-ordinated zoning applied to planning
is seen to have the following policy implications for the Countryside Around
Towns:-

a) recognition of the strategic importance of the green belt as reinforcing the
regional strategy of urban renewal and not merely as a measure of environmental
protection (authors emphasis);

b) to require local plans in the green belt to include policies and proposals
for the management of urban fringe pressures;

c) to give priority to the management of urban fringe pressures in a pilot study
area (see Conurbation Key Diagram) and seek joint initiatives with the District
Council, the SDA and the Countryside Commission;

d) formalise the general presumption against isolated development in the wider
area of countryside around towns, outwith the green belt.
SRC(1981c)

A pilot study of the management of urban fringe pressures such as that proposed
in the Newton area of Strathclyde is urgently required in Scotland. What is the
status of agriculture in the urban fringe in Scotland? The general picture of
advantages and problems appears to be much as elsewhere but without surveys
similar to those carried out in Tyne and Wear, Dernie, White and Jolliffe (1976)
Essex, Blair (1980) and the London Green Belt, Munton(1981) peculiarly Scottish
characteristics remain unidentified. For example are 'hobby' farming and part-
time farming OECD (1978) Fuguitt et al (1977) Fuller & Mage (1979) Layton (1978)
as significant as elsewhere or did the creation of consolidated and relatively
large agricultural units in the 18th and 19th centuries in the peri-urban areas
of Scotland result in an ownership and tenancy pattern which does not introduce
small acreage units to the land market, or are they usually the product of
fragmentation brought about by urban development?

Burrows' study, Burrows (1978), Philips & Veal (1979) p.46 produced evidence from
Birmingham, Liverpool and Glasgow that two thirds or more of the vacant land in
urban areas (i.e. Local Authority Districts) is not found in the inner-city but
peripherally on the urban fringe, around ten per cent of the land there being
vacant. Any attempt at management of the fringe will require detailed knowledge
of the amount, location and characteristics of such vacant land. Ray Bleasdale
(Chapter 5) states that a knowledge of the amount of derelict land is not important
as it is always changing. It is true that one man's junk yard may be another's
idea of an antique collection or 'op art' display but the collection and maintenance of a data bank recording land use in our peri-urban areas, particularly on
the urban fringe is surely essential to the management of such areas. The Strathclyde proposals are to look to joint initiatives with other authorities including
the SDA and the Countryside Commission for Scotland in any fringe area management
schemes. Decisions regarding priority areas for action will surely be made after
survey. Alastaire Gilchrist's paper (Chapter 5) demonstrates some of the
technical possibilities in the rahabilitation of derelict land and in so doing
surely reminds land use planners of their role in diagnosing appropriate future
use of currently derelict land.

On a broader front, Ken McDonald (Chapter 4) discusses an analysis of the countryside around towns in the major urbanised area of Central Region, Scotland. The
procedure followed by the consultants employed was one of brief survey followed
by identification of projects, the detailed information required before action
to be gathered when required and where required. This methodology highlights
a failing in survey techniques employed to date - they are too time consuming
with the result that by completion date the circumstances have changed to a

significant degree. In the researching of new survey methods combining accuracy
with speed lies a major challenge for the academic disciplines concerned.

The Central Scotland Woodlands Project which is discussed by both Ken McDonald
and Graham Jeffrey (Chapter 6) demonstrates the possibilities of one type of
management scheme,Edwards (1979) Sheldon (1980) and highlights the role of project
officers and the economic problems inherent in small scale woodlands and copses,
Row (1978). Hopefully management methods such as community woodlands or recreational woodlands will ensure that the value of small woodlands to landscape
and society as described by Crowe (1979) is realised. Were the Strathclyde
designation of Countryside Around Towns applied to equivalent areas throughout
Central Scotland (MacIver 1979) then several forests would lie within the
encompassed area, and also within designated Regional Scenic Areas.The management
of such forests to allow them to play an integrated role in the recreational
facilities of the peri-urban area may reduce the financial return on capital
investment. However, it is to be hoped that even in a period of economic recession Central Government will see fit to allow the Forestry Commission who
clearly appreciate the possibilities, Montgomery (1981) to pursue such management
policies where appropriate. What inducements if any are required to induce
private forest interests to follow similar multi-use management policies?

Seldom can there have been such an influential and seminal document as the
Dartington Amenity Trust Study, The Countryside around Towns in Scotland DART
(1976). Its influence on the thinking of the Countryside Commission for Scotland
is very evident from Thomas Huxley's paper (Chapter 2) while its wider significance
is testified to by the number of references to it in this and other volumes
concerned with the peri-urban areas. John Mackay (Chapter 3) demonstrates some
of the ways it has influenced both the research directions and actions of the
Countryside Commission for Scotland in the field of recreation.

Countryside in Scotland accommodates a multiplicity of recreational activities
and a mobile host of participants in a manner unknown in other long settled or
property conscious countries of the developed world. The Scot has inherited a
singular attitude, some would say rights, to access to the countryside. As
recreational pressures increase this is leading to questioning of attitudes and
reassessment of rights. As was pointed out at the Symposium the pressures are
as yet far below those being experienced in England thus affording time to evolve
strategies and policies ahead of crisis conditions. Recreation in the countryside
is cast as villain by many and saviour by few, Shand (1976).

In Scotland, in Victorian times, excluding hunting lodges, second homes were
largely confined to areas which had become peri-urban as a result of the development of the rail and steamer network and could be reached in less than one hour's
travelling time. It is a commentary on our times that some of these areas in
Strathclyde Region are now classified as 'Remote Rural'. Today the villages of the
peri-urban areas in Scotland as in other developed countries are under pressure
to accommodate those who commute to work in the urban areas and second homes have
been pushed to the outer edges of the peri-urban area or beyond, Boyer (1980).
Development which has been largely in the form of small housing estates constructed
by developers, has dramatically changed the character of such villages in the rural
west of Central Region as it has done in many peri-urban areas. In general the
response of planning authorities to continuing pressure for further development
has been to severely limit further development. Is such an attitude an admission
of failure? Must further development of a village already drastically changed
physically and socially be unacceptable in form? The Age of Improvement saw
the erection of numerous villages in Scotland to which today 'conservation area'
status is given. Is there not need, are there not suitable sites where the

conservation villages of next century could be built in this decade?

Environmental constraints

In this volume Joy Tivy draws attention to the part played by smaller water bodies in recreational activity in Central Scotland. In the publication Water in Scotland SDD (1980a) it is stated that Scotland's rivers are relatively clean, a survey in 1975 having revealed that only 1.3% were regarded as being of poor quality or grossly polluted. An environmental conservationist or a keen angler based in Central Scotland might view the situation differently.

Two decades after the creation of the River Purification Boards, and despite their best efforts and considerable success some strategically located streams in the peri-urban areas of Scotland are still grossly polluted and others although of reasonable biological standard detract rather than contribute to amenity. Ian Nicholson's paper (Chapter 9) serves as a reminder not only of the need to monitor impacts on the peri-urban environment but also that appreciation of the critical levels of pollution changes with advances in research techniques.

While it may be agreed that evaluation of landscape value is an art rather than the science many tried to make it Penning-Roswell (1981) this does not reduce the need for such value judgments in planning. For example in Gwent one of the three broad areas in which countryside management is seen as being required is 'areas of high landscape value', Probert & Hamersley (1979).

The range of environmental constraints is wide emphasising once again the continuing role of the peri-urban areas as the loci of interactions. Even past interactions, be they evidenced by archaeological remains or mining subsidence serve as restraints on present development.

CONCLUSION

This symposium, it is hoped, has gone some way to disarming the criticism that, 'the countryside is a unity, but it is planned by a disparate variety of individuals and organisations, often experts in their own field, yet ignorant of other forces which may fundamentally affect their own long term objectives.' Gilg (1981). The range of papers presented confirms that initiatives related to the problems and possibilities of peri-urban areas are not lacking in Scotland and that there are ample opportunities for further contributions.

REFERENCES

A.E.I.C.O.(1944) Agricultural Economies Research Unit. Country Planning, OUP London
Allison, L. (1978). In defence of virgin land New Society 45 (823) pp. 64-66.
Best, R.H.(1976a). The changing land-use structure of Britain. Town & Country Planning 44(3) pp. 171-176.
Best, R.H. (1976b). The extent and growth of urban land in Britain. The Planner. 62 pp. 8-11.
Best, R.H. (1977) Agricultural land loss - myth or reality. The Planner. 63(1) pp. 15-16.
Best, R.H. (1979). Land use structure and change in the EEC. Town Planning Review. 50, pp. 395-411.
Blacksell, M. (1979). Landscape protection and development control: an appraisal of planning in rural areas of England and Wales. Geoforum 10(3) pp.267-274.
Blair, A.M. (1980). Urban Influences in Farming in Essex. Geoforum 10 (3) pp.371-384.
Boyer, J.C. (1980). Second Homes and 'urbanization' in the Paris Region. Tijdschrift v Economische wn Sociale Geographie 71(2) pp. 78-87.

Burrows, J. (1978). Vacant Urban Land. The Planner, 64, 1. pp.7-9.
Coleman, A. (1977). Land use planning: success or failure. Architects' Journal,
    165 (a) pp.387-388.
Coppock, J.T. (1977). The challenge of change: problems of rural land use in
    Great Britain. Geography 62(2) pp. 75-86.
Crowe, S. (1979). The value of small woodlands to landscape and society. Parks
    4(1) pp.5-7.
DART (1976). Dartington Amenity Research Trust. The Countryside and Towns in
    Scotland. CCS unpublished 1976.
Davidson, J. & Wibberley, C. (1977). Planning and the rural environment.
    Pergamon Press. Urban and Regional Planning Series Vol. 18.
Dernie, P.J., White, C.F. & Jolliffe, W. (1976). Agriculture in the urban fringe.
    A survey in the Metropolitan County of Tyne and Wear. Technical Report,
    Agricultural Development and Advisory Service, 30(1).
Diamond, D.R. (1979). The uses of strategic planning: the example of the natural
    planning guidelines in Scotland. Town Planning Review. 50(1) pp. 18-25.
Edwards, C. (1979) Central Scotland Woodlands Project. Landscape Design. 128
    pp.20-22.
Elson, M. (1976). Recreation, green belts and Green Belt Locale Plans. Oxford
    Polytechnic, Dept. of Town Planning 1976. Working Paper No. 38. pp.34-72.
Elson, M. (1981a). Farmland loss and the erosion of planning. Town and Country
    Planning, 1981, 1, pp.20-21.
Elson, M. (1981b). Structure Plan Policies for Pressured Rural Areas pp. 49-70
    in Gilg, A.W. (ed.) Countryside Planning Yearbook 1981 Geo. Books. Norwich.
Fugitt, G., Fuller, A., Fuller, H., Gasson, R., & Jones, C. Part-time farming:
    its nature and implications: a workshop report. Centre for European Agricul-
    tural Studies, Wye College, Seminar Paper 2.
Fuller, A.M. & Mage, J.A. (eds.) (1979). Part-time farming: Problem of resource
    in rural development. Geo. Books Norwich.
Gardner, K., Bills, N. Lesher, N., Cobb, K., Allee, D. (1977). New York's agricul-
    tural districts. The preservation of farming rather than the restriction
    of growth. Cornell Agricultural Economics Staff Paper. Dept. of Ag.Econ.
    Cornell University, 77-16. 24 pp.
Gilg, A.W. (1978). Disappearing land: speculation or fact. Farmers Weekly, 89(1)
    p.98.
Gilg, A.W. (1980). Planning for Rural Employment in a changed economy. The Planner.
    66 No. 4. pp.91-92.
Gilg, A.W. (ed.) (1981). Countryside Planning Yearbook 1981 Geo. Books. Norwich.
Hart, S.F. (1976). Urban Encroachment in Rural Areas. Geog. Rev. 66(1) pp.1-12.
Hebbert, M. (1979). Green Belt problem of the Farmer. Oxford Polytechnic Dept.
    of Town Planning. Working Paper No. 38. p.87.
Hebbert, M. (1981). The land debate and the planning system. Town and Country
    Planning, 1981. 1. pp.22-23.
Hovinen, G.R. (1977). Leapfrog developments in Lancaster County. Professional
    Geographer 29(2) pp.194-199.
JURUE (1977). Planning and Land Availability: a study on behalf of the DoE.
    Joint Unit for Research in the Urban Environment. The University of Aston
    in Birmingham.
Lapping, M.B. (1975). Preserving agricultural lands: the New York experience.
    Town and Country Planning 43(9), 394-397.
Layton, R.L. (1978). The operational structure of the hobby farm. Area, 10(4)
    1978. pp.242-246.
Lievesley, K. (ed.) (1976). The Community Land Act. Regional Studies Association
    Discussion Paper 8. 1976. 36 pp.
MacIver, I.F. (1979). Forestry in central Scotland. Forestry, 52(1) pp.91-100.
Manning, E.W. & McCuaig, J.D. (1977). Agricultural land and urban centres: a
    review of the significance of urban centres to Canada's quality agricultural
    land. Lands Directorate, Canada Land Inventory. Report I. 32 pp.

Merchant, M. (1976). The gap between pattern and plan. Surveyor 148 (4389) 1976.
    pp. 14-15.
Montgomery, Sir D. (1981). Forestry and the Environment. pp. 84-86 in Gilg, A.W.,
    (ed.) Countryside Planning Yearbook. Geo. Books. Norwich 1981.
Morris, D.E. (1977). Farmland values and urbanization. Agricultural Economics
    Research 20(1) pp. 44-47.
Moss, G. (1981). Land Council and its Objectives. Town and Country Planning
        50 No. 1 pp. 11-13.
Munton, R. (1981). Agricultural land use in the London Greenbelt. Town and Country
    Planning.   50 No. 1. pp.17-19.
OECD (1979) Agriculture in the planning and management of peri-urban areas.
    Organisation for Economic Co-operation and Development, Paris 1979. 94 pages.
OECD (1976). Land Use Policies and Agriculture. Chap. 2 Paris 1976. OECD. 1979.
OECD (1978). Part Time Farming in OECD Countries. OECD Agricultural Policy Reports
    Paris 1978.
Penning-Rowsell, E.C. (1981). Fluctuating fortunes in gauging landscape value.
    Progress in Human Geog. V5. No. 1. pp 25-41.
Phillips, J.C. and Veal, A.J. (1979). Research on the Urban Fringe. University of
    Birmingham, 1979. Report of a Countryside Commission Seminar 1978. Centre
    for Urban and Regional Studies.
Pierce, J.T. (1979). Land conversion and urban growth, Canada 1946-71.
    Tijdschrift v Ecm. in Soc. Geog. 70, 333-338.
Pierce, J.T. (1981). Conversion of rural land to urban: or Canadian profile.
    Professional Geographer. 33(2) pp. 163-173.
Platt, R.H. (1981). Farmland Conversion: National Lessons for Iowa. Professional
    Geographer. 33. No. 1. pp 113-121.
Probert, C. and Hammersley, C. (1979). Countryside Management in Gwent. The Planner
    65(1), pp. 10-13.
Rogers, A.W. (ed.) (1978). Urban growth, farmland losses and planning: a
    symposium. Wye College, Ashford, Kent, Countryside Planning Unit 65.
Row, C. (1978). Economies of tract size in timber growing. J. of Forestry, 76 (9)
    pp. 576-582.
Scottish Development Department (1980). Agricultural Land and Urban Development
    Central Planning Group, Unpublished Report. SDD January 1980. 29.
Scottish Development Department (1980a). Water in Scotland: a review. HMSO
    Publication.
Shand, M. (1976). Recreation: the key to the survival of England's countryside.
    in Future landscapes, ed. W. MacEwen (Chatto & Windus) London.
Sheldon, J. (1980). The Central Scotland Woodlands Project: a plan for land use
    and landscape renewal. Arboricultural Journal. 4, pp. 41-49.
SRC (1981). Strathclyde Structure Plan. First Review and Alteration, Consultative
    Draft, Strathclyde Regional Council, Glasgow 1981. 141 pages. SRC (1981a) op cit
    p. 22 SRC (1981b) op cit p. 47 SRC (1981c) op cit p. 42.
Thompson, K.J. (1977). Agricultural change and conservation in the Urban Fringe.
    Report for the Countryside Commission. Dept. of Agric. Econ. Newcastle upon Tyne.
Vining, D.R., Bieri, K. & Strauss, A. (1977). Urbanization of prime agricultural
    land in the U.S. A statistical analysis. Regional Science Research Institute.
    (RSR 1) Discussion Paper Series. 99. 41 pp.
Wibberley, C.P. (1976). Competing demands for land. Farm Management 3(9) pp.222-228.
Wibberley, C. (1981). Recent change in land use and agricultural realities. Town
    and Country Planning, V 50, No. 1. pp. 13-15.

Fig. 2.1 SCOTLAND'S COUNTRY PARKS

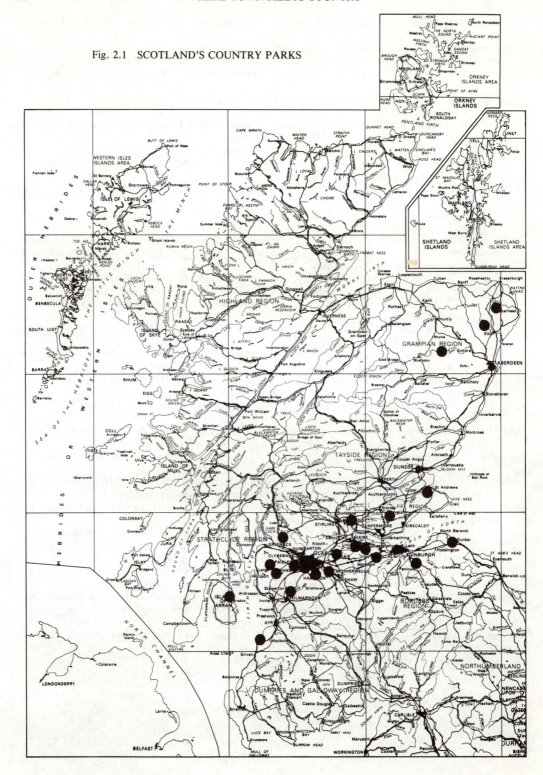

CHAPTER 2

THE COUNTRYSIDE COMMISSION FOR SCOTLAND'S WORK IN THE COUNTRYSIDE AROUND
TOWNS OF SCOTLAND

Thomas Huxley
Deputy Director

ABSTRACT

Having briefly reviewed the work of the Commission as a whole, the paper explains
how 'countryside' came to be defined and why this is relevant to the Commission's
work in peri-urban areas. The development of the Commission's interest in the
countryside around towns is then presented, and the contribution of a report by
the Dartington Amenity Research Trust briefly explained as an introduction to the
next two symposium papers illustrating how some of the ideas proposed by DART have
been taken forward. The reason for lack of progress on one of the DART report's
proposals is also explained and the paper concludes with some speculation as to
the way in which the Commission's interest and role in peri-urban areas will continue
in future.

KEYWORDS

Countryside Commission for Scotland; definition of countryside; the countryside
around towns; DART Report; evaluation of benefit.

In all its activities throughout the countryside of Scotland, there are five key
words which characterise the Commission's work. They are: protection, provision,
research, education and review. Protection relates to duties to advise the Secretary of State and local authorities about developments under the planning acts
and the contents of structure and local plans in terms of countryside policies.
Provision relates to giving grant for informal recreational provisions and enhancement of amenity. Education relates to improving understanding and behaviour.
Research as a term is clear enough, the important supplementary point for the
Commission is that research is linked to special powers to carry out development
projects. Finally, review: although this is arguably part of each of the above,
we like to identify it as an activity of importance in its own right.

Because all five of these activities are practiced everywhere within designated
countryside (see below), it follows that examples could be given of the particular
form which they take in peri-urban areas. Details could be given of the kinds of
observations the Commission planning staff make on development plans and on specific
planning consultations. Likewise, the kinds of schemes on which they - often jointly
with staff in the Conservation Education Branch - recommend grant, ranging from
country parks (most of which are located close to towns - Fig. 2.1) and visitor

13

Fig. 2.2   DESIGNATED COUNTRYSIDE: SAMPLE MAP

centres to tree planting schemes, could be described. This however is an intro-
ductory paper to the Commission's research and development activities, with an
emphasis on policy and cannot detail the Commission's advisory and funding work,
notwithstanding its importance.

But first, there is a definitional matter which must be explained. This is done
by adopting an historical approach (as elsewhere in this paper), thereby enabling
the reader not only to be presented with an idea but also the development of
thinking leading to it. In the mid-sixties, the author was the former Nature
Conservancy's Assessor to a committee set up by the Secretary of State for Scotland,
the report of which subsequently led to the Countryside (Scotland) Act 1967 and
the creation of the Countryside Commission for Scotland. The government of the
day, having accepted that it would draft a Bill, the committee was twice recalled
to give its views on various matters relevant to that task. The first of these
concerned a definition of countryside and the committee was chided for not having
so done in its report. The members had thought this irrelevant, believing that
there was a continuum from town to country and that legislation should not be
introduced in an attempt to distinguish where one stopped and the other commenced.

The civil servants, however, were much exercised that the limited funds to be made
available by the new legislation would be largely absorbed by the big cities. They
therefore wrote into the Act the concept of 'countryside' and laid upon the Secretary of State the duty of preparing detailed maps designating that which would be
'countryside'. The Act specified certain factors to be taken into account - such
as whether the land was of a rural character and its suitability for open-air
recreation - to which the Secretary of State added other considerations - such as
the population size of settlements to be excluded from countryside. There were
consultations too with the former planning authorities, some of whom amongst the
cities and larger burghs were more and some less keen to have parts of their areas
so designated - in accordance with the extent to which they saw the Act as providing opportunities or constraints on their activities. Suffice it to say that almost
as soon as the maps were published, tiny bits became out of date so that now -
despite a few amending designations (all including as countryside that which orig-
inally has been excluded) - the much quoted statement that 98.5% of Scotland is
countryside no longer holds strictly true.

This historical explanation has been given because it is in the peri-urban areas
that its consequences are of greatest importance. This is the area where the maps
of designated countryside must be frequently consulted, so as to verify the
Commission's competence to give advice and money. To a degree, however, the fact
of designation is increasingly working in the Commission's favour. It can be
seen why, most clearly, by looking to England and Wales, where the Countryside Act
of 1968 did not introduce a procedure for designating countryside. The effect of
this is that our sister Commission is continually having to assess whether schemes
are appropriate for countryside grant, in terms of perceived criteria for countryside. By and large, the Commission for Scotland does not have to go through that
process; all that is required is to consult the maps - an example is shown in
Map 2 - and, as actual physical town spreads out into actual countryside, leaving
the designated boundary where drawn over a decade ago, the Commission's interests
are increasingly able to penetrate into the urban end of the town to country
continuum.

In giving perspective to the Commission's interests in peri-urban areas, it is
convenient to move back, both in space and time, to the period just before the
Commission was established and to the Secretary of State's committee mentioned
earlier. No doubt the range of views was as varied as the membership but the
author does not think he was alone in expecting that the new body would have to
give high priority to the central belt, close to where most people lived in

Scotland. Partly this was because, at that time, the Highlands and Islands
Development Board had just been set up, so it looked as if funding in the
Highland areas would come largely from the Board. The subsequent growth in
visitor numbers to remote rural areas had barely begun and likewise recognition
of the necessity for schemes both to provide for enjoyment of countryside and
for its protection. Then too, in 1967, North Sea Oil still lay below the horizon
of most people's awareness, along with all the subsequent heavy demands on the
Commission's staff resources to appraise and comment on these new massive developments.

In the early years of the Commission, it thus came to the author as something of
a surprise to discover how widely dispersed the Commission's activities were.
This was not just in response to demands from local authorities; both members
and senior colleagues saw a need for the Commission to establish itself across the
whole geography of Scotland and with the greater wisdom of hindsight, the author
can now see how right that policy was. Indeed, to a degree, that policy must
always obtain. Unlike both the Scottish Tourist Board and Scottish Sports Council,
and of course also the HIDB, the Commission does not have an investment policy
which gives preference to some areas of Scottish countryside over others, and the
author does not see this happening in the future, so long as the basic legislative
structure of our activities stays the same.

Nevertheless, over the years, there has been a growing awareness of the need to
give special consideration to what the Commission has called 'The Countryside
Around Towns'. One source of that growing awareness was the Commission's consultative paper published in 1974 on a 'Park System for Scotland' wherein a recreational system for Scotland is described. In Chapter 4 it states: 'the full scope
of outdoor recreation reaches from the back garden and local urban play area to
remote country possessing high wilderness value' and, in the next chapter, a park
system was described ranging from urban parks through country parks and regional
parks to special parks.

In this way, the existence of urban needs, as part of a spectrum of needs, became
recognised in Commission policy, albeit that a special value attaching to peri-
urban areas as such did not surface in the aforementioned consultative report.
Nevertheless the first relevant reference to a specific interest in the countryside
around towns also dates to 1974 when a Commission staff review of research needs
was conducted. This exercise listed several ideas broadly concerned with recreational provision in the Central Belt of Scotland some of which were linked to other
suggestions concerned with environmental improvement, especially in the countryside
around towns.

The following year these underlined words became the common title of two further
papers considered by the Commission. One recommended expenditure on a situation
report on Scotland's Green Belts and the other, a report to be prepared by the
Dartington Amenity Research Trust, of which more shortly. The situation report
on green belts was subsequently prepared by David Skinner and has become a
valuable point of departure between the Commission and the local authorities on
green belt policies. 1975 was also important because it was the year when the
Countryside Recreation Research Advisory Group (an advisory group chaired by our
sister Commission made up of central and local government agencies) chose as the
theme for its autumn conference 'Recreation and the Urban Fringe'.

The DART report, entitled 'The Countryside Around Towns in Scotland' was at that
time for the Commission a novel type of report in which to invest. Rather than
research some particular subject area, DART was invited to undertake a desk study
on the potential of the countryside around towns for research and experiment, with
particular regard to research on environmental conservation and informal outdoor

Fig. 2.3 THE COUNTRYSIDE AROUND TOWNS IN SCOTLAND

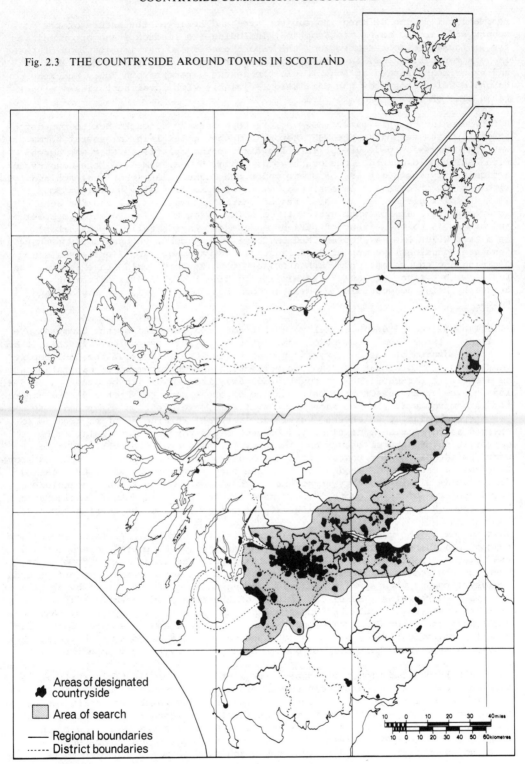

Areas of designated countryside

Area of search

Regional boundaries

District boundaries

recreation. Having defined its subject area and reviewed the nature of the
countryside around towns in Scotland, including its landscape and opportunities
for informal outdoor recreation, the report considered the implications of these
factors for policy and, in a final chapter, drew out 12 proposals for research
and experiment (Listed at Annex). In the next two papers John Mckay and Ken
McDonald write about how the Commission - jointly with local authorities - have
taken some of these ideas forward.

Before concluding this paper, however, it is necessary to backtrack to two definitional points regarding the DART report and then to explain in general terms the
way the Commission made use of it. The first point relates to what was agreed
with DART should comprise the countryside around towns, namely: "the countryside
designated by the Secretary of State under the Countryside (Scotland) Act and lying
within five, or normally at most ten, miles of a major built-up area in Scotland."
This definition resulted in the 'area of search' shown in Map 2 and the author is
interested to learn to what extent it coincides with the views of this symposium
and others as to the extent of peri-urban areas. Incidentally, 'peri-urban'
is a term which has never been used in Commission papers, unconsciously perhaps as
just not sounding like our kind of language. It was, however, a quite conscious
decision not to use the term 'urban fringe' because this could have led to con-
fusion with a range of activities similar in kind but obviously different in
geography being conducted by our sister Countryside Commission in England and
Wales.

Although the second definitional point has not been promoted by the Commission -
or anyone else - it may yet be of some interest to this symposium. In their chapter
on the landscape of the countryside around towns, the authors of the DART report
considered the idea that whereas the protection and enhancement of natural beauty
is a fairly clear-cut issue in countryside away from towns, it becomes a good deal
less clear-cut in the Central Belt because of the extent to which its rural character is compromised. In the face of this dilemma, the question was posed:
"Is there a point at which the 'rural' or 'natural' character of an area is so
changed as to provide a distinctly different basis for decisions relating to
conservation of natural beauty and amenity?" The authors thought such a point
could be identified and that, within the countryside around towns as defined above,
there was a category of land other than the towns themselves, which they called
'countryside within the city structure'. They even went so far as to include a
tentative map which, to quote, "would need further and more formal consideration
by Government and local authorities" if the concept were to be carried forward.

Turning now to the use made of the DART report, the Commission's first action was
to set up a number of carefully structured meetings with central government and
the relevant local authorities, to whom the report was circulated. From these
meetings the Commission drew out a priority list for action, in terms of research
and development, with specific additions being made to the DART list by certain of
the local authorities. Since publication of the report in December 1976, it would
be fair to say that about three-quarters of the suggestions proposed by DART have
been taken up by the Commission one way or another and thus - subject to various
detailed qualifications most of which need not concern us today - the report has
proved to be an important seminal document in precisely the way hoped of it.

One general qualification must however be mentioned. This is that, while it is
difficult under any circumstances to make proposals for research and action which
will be generally thought intelligent and sensible and which are really worthwhile
taking up, it can be another order of difficulty altogether to make suggestions
that can be acted upon by the Commission in terms of its statutory powers and
technical and other resources. Thus a few of the suggestions in the DART report
have not been taken forward because the organisations who would have to be

involved - including the Commission - have deemed the suggestions impracticable and significantly more than any other, this difficulty attaches to the last of the DART proposals, concerning the radical restructuring of land use and landscape in the countryside around towns.

What the authors had in mind involved the re-shaping of farms, planting of shelter-belts, re-shaping of road and footpath systems, clearance of derelict land and other action. They thought that several of the other studies proposed by them might throw light on the issues at stake and this has proved correct, especially in the Central Scotland Woodlands Project which Ken McDonald writes about in this volume. The authors of the report believed, however, that after an initial period of research and experiment, it should be possible to identify a suitable area in which to undertake a practical experiment in the restructuring of land, involving collaboration between the local authorities, landowners and government agencies, including the Commission.

It would be fair to ask why this proposal has not been taken up, even to the extent of looking without commitment for a possible suitable area? The answer does not lie in the idea per se being foolish. During the course of the symposium many participants probably came to a similar conclusion and may suggest that if significant improvements are to be made to the countryside around towns, in terms of productive land use and appearance, solutions must begin by tackling such fundamental difficulties as land use and land use structure. So the reasons for lack of progress must lie elsewhere.

Probably top of the list is lack of political will. Both elected members and those who elect them are willing to accept considerable personal inconvenience and disruption for the purposes of building major new roads, new towns or advance factories. That willingness is often forthcoming, of course, because it is bought at a high price of costly litigation and compensation. Complex projects, however, are achieved not just by political will and public acceptance but also by inter-organisational and/or inter-departmental collaboration. Thus the political will must and does go even further, for certain purposes, by setting up special bodies - such as New Town Corporations - and in this way enjoining powerful departments of state, each used to going its own way, to collaborate one with the other. But projects relating to land between major developments do not generally carry the same degree of political will and consequently everything becomes more difficult and more uncertain, except the certainty of needing infinite patience.

In concluding this paper, it might be helpful to the symposium if something definite was written about future Commission policy in regard to peri-urban areas. At best, however, the author can only speculate, noting first some possibilities which seem to be unlikely. One mentioned earlier: the unlikelihood of the Commission itself determining some strongly beneficial investment policies (across the full width of its activities) for the countryside around towns, at the expense of other parts of Scotland. Nevertheless, inasmuch as country parks are mostly located in peri-urban areas (see Map 3) and because they take up roughly half our grant giving ability to be responsive to local need, countryside near where most people live in Scotland will still be a major beneficiary of Countryside Act funds.

Another unlikely happening - both in terms of grant and its powers to spend money through development projects - is that the Commission will ever become the major source of funds for repairing the ravages of past industries, clearing derelict land etc. It will, of course, continue to act where appropriate as a stimulant, to provide a co-ordinating service and to make some financial resources available. The really big funds, however, will always be likely to come from other bodies, such as central government and the local authorities themselves through the Rate

Support Grant and from specially created bodies such as the Scottish Development Agency.

Nevertheless, it is the author's expectation that the Commission will seek to continue to be identified strongly with certain problems in peri-urban areas, not just because such problems are demanding of and appropriate to the Commission's attention, but also because it is in the local authorities of the Central Belt that the political need for the Commission is most unanimously expressed and least in debate. It makes good political sense to help those who appreciate being helped!

There is, however, a policy-related research question an answer to which the author is less able to provide with confidence. The type of research in question is really a string of related research problems, all at bottom concerned with investigating the extent to which people actually benefit - or fail to benefit - from Countryside Act investment in recreational provision. There is no long-standing tradition for carrying out such research; the development of the splendid series of city parks over the past hundred years in Glasgow, Edinburgh, Aberdeen and Dundee, was achieved without anyone feeling the need for surveys to demonstrate or justify such actions. Measures of success were obtained without statistics and a deep seated distrust as to their value is still widespread.

Nevertheless, although having some sympathy with the thought that the case for needing good statistical information has yet to be proved, the author is sure it is right that the Commission should continue to invest some of its research funds in this subject area especially because, if we do not take the lead, no one else will. But in doing so, the effort must not just be directed at improving the quality of the research. An equal effort will have to be made to demonstrate the real value of such research for decision making, both at the political and management levels.

SUMMARY OF PROPOSALS IN DART REPORT

1. Study of the incidence, effects and possible treatment of urban 'efflux'.

2. Monitoring of users selected urban parks and country parks.

3. Experiments in management of urban fringe areas.

4. A study of access systems in the countryside around towns.

5. A study of people's perceptions of landscape character and of recreational opportunities and settings.

6. Study/experiment in the role of public transport in informal outdoor recreation.

7. Study/experiment in community involvement in landscape management/ recreational provision.

8. Study/experiment in 'nature-assisted' management of recreational areas.

9. Study/experiment in links between farming and recreation in the countryside around towns.

10. Study of the potential role of new woodland planting in the countryside around towns.

11. Experiment in the extended use of powers related to derelict land.

12. Study/experiment in the radical restructuring of land use and landscape in the countryside within the city structure.

CHAPTER 3
RECREATION IN THE COUNTRYSIDE AROUND TOWNS

John W. Mackay
Countryside Commission for Scotland

ABSTRACT

This paper begins with a brief review of four projects, all concerned with informal
recreation close to towns and sponsored by the Countryside Commission for Scotland
in collaboration with several local authorities as part of the Commission's research
and development programme in the countryside around towns. Some general results are
drawn from the projects and these are discussed in a wider context of current
thinking about recreation provision close to towns.

KEYWORDS

Countryside around towns; outdoor recreation; Countryside Commission; Union Canal;
Lomond Hills; access to countryside; recreational transport services; impacts.

INTRODUCTION

It is now well accepted in land-use planning for countryside close to towns that
such land has an important role to play in providing space for outdoor recreation
by townsfolk. There is nothing particularly novel about this notion. Its historical roots in Scotland may lie in the town muir or common land of burghs, which
served as a resort for public recreation. At a later stage parks, often at the
edge of towns, were created by the city corporation and burgh authorities of the
last century. It is of interest that not all of these new developments were parks
in the formal sense. The origin of Cathkin Braes Park on the south side of Glasgow
was a private benefaction in 1886 by a Mr. James Dick, an industrialist who had
long admired the beauties of the spot. In terms of that gift it is onjoined,
"... that the natural features and configuration of the round be maintained ...
that the public be permitted to roam at will ... that football, cricket and similar
sports shall be strictly prohibited". Here is a vision of refreshment and recreation taken in harmony with the natural features of countryside, a country park
a few miles from the then existing edge of the city, long before the idea of
country park was formalised in legislation. Later, the linkage between the
recreation needs of urban residents and the opportunities on land close to towns
was brought into the green belt concept, and more recently this general message
has been reiterated formally through a range of channels, such as structure plan
policies and in regional strategies prepared under the Scottish Tourism and

Fig. 3.1 RESEARCH AND DEVELOPMENT PROJECTS IN THE COUNTRYSIDE AROUND TOWNS

Recreation Planning Studies (STARPS) programme.

In the wider debate which has developed in recent years, (about land use close to towns), considerable interest has been focused on problems in the urban fringe and this has led to much research, review and policy formulation, some of which has been concerned with recreational issues. This short paper is concerned with recreation and it has two main aims, first to report briefly on research and development projects undertaken recently by the Countryside Commission for Scotland relating to recreation in the countryside around towns and second, to tease out some general issues from the Commission's and other relevant research work and to tilt gently at some existing thinking on recreation provision around towns. This paper is written from a viewpoint that takes a liberal view - in terms of distance - of countryside around towns (DART, 1976) rather than a narrow girdle at the edge of the built up area. Also, this paper approaches recreation largely in terms that the Commission is primarily concerned with, under the general label of informal recreation, that is walking, viewing, picnicking and driving.

Four Recreational Projects

The preceding paper describes the approach taken by the Countryside Commission for Scotland in seeking to focus part of its research and development effort on issues concerning the countryside around towns, namely, the commissioning from the Dartington Amenity Research Trust of a general research review as a starting point for discussion with other interested parties. Quite soon, after receipt of this report (DART 1976), six research initiatives were launched and mostly co-sponsored in collaboration with local authorities in the central belt of Scotland. Only in small part did these new projects exactly mirror the proposals made by the consultant. However, the generality of what was undertaken drew heavily from DART's twelve themes. Four of the six projects were concerned with recreation issues and they have either been completed recently or are close to completion. The other two had a strong landscape theme and they are discussed in the subsequent paper. All six projects are located on Figure 3:1.

The first recreational project concerned monitoring of the use of parks, involving comprehensive recreational surveys of five important parks, all located on the southern side of the Glasgow conurbation. This work was undertaken in three consecutive studies mounted between 1977 and 1979 in co-sponsorship, variously, with Strathclyde Regional Council and the City of Glasgow District Council and the surveys were all contracted to the Tourism and Recreation Research Unit of the University of Edinburgh (TRRU).

These are important studies on two general counts: first they provide a most comprehensive set of data about the detailed use of parks close to and within towns. Second, when added to the now substantial body of existing information about the use of rural recreation sites, these new surveys significantly widen our knowledge of the spatial, the temporal, and the social aspects of this aspect of leisure. Full reports of the surveys have been published by TRRU in the Unit's Research Report Series (TRRU, 1978, 1980a, 1980b) and these reports warrant close examination by anyone interested in recreation in parks.

The other three projects were mounted as development projects (under Section 5 of the Countryside (Scotland) Act) which involves the practical demonstration of an idea or technique, often as a follow-up to a previous research study. The Commission always seeks to apply a large input of research methodology to these projects, in commissioning small-scale research studies to underpin the direct action and, in monitoring the outcome of action under the project. Such projects are run on fairly small budgets, with the main resource applied to the work being a human one, a project officer, whose role is to act as a pioneer or entrepreneur or promotor on behalf of his or her project theme. Implicit in the demonstrating of something innovative is the hope that the work of the project will be converted into some more permanent arrangement and that the original idea will commend itself to a wider audience.

The Commission, Central and Lothian Regional Councils and the British Waterways Board collaborated in the first such project which was concerned to promote the recreational use of the Union Canal, the remainder waterway, located between Falkirk and Edinburgh and owned by the Board. This is a canal of considerable historical interest, sadly having its navigation broken in several places by roadworks and housing development undertaken since the end of commercial use of the waterway. It is still attractive for recreation and conveniently located for such use. It is in public ownership, with the local authorities and the Board interested in seeing this recreational potential further developed, and there is a very lively group of voluntary canal clubs and societies. Thus, the prime aim of the Union Canal project was promotional, to build on existing goodwill, to generate awareness of and interest in the canal and to encourage its use by public at large. After two years of this special stimulus, the project phase has ended and arrangements are being discussed for the work to be absorbed by the local authorities in some more permanent arrange- ment. It is too soon to evaluate the Union Canal Project as much will depend on the extent to which the initial impetus is sustained. A base-line survey has been carried out to provide comparison with re-survey at some later date (CCS, 1981a).

The next project was less straightforward. Titled the Lomond Hills Project, its main theme was to explore a range of issues on the theme of access to the country- side. This project is co-sponsored with Fife Regional Council. It operates within a project area of some 50 square miles including the Lomond Hills, sensu stricto, (and thereby overlapping the regional boundary into Tayside Region) and an adjoining area of central Fife to the south, including the old mining villages from Lochgelly to Ballingry, and it abuts the edge of Glenrothes New Town. The project area was chosen so as to delimit a piece of countryside with a diversity of land uses, settle- ment types and recreational activities that exemplify situations to be found else- where in central Scotland, where industrial towns are located close to open hill land. It was also not too large for a project officer to cope with in a project of relatively short duration.

The Lomond Hills project took a broad view of access to the countryside, being concerned with the physical means of access such as the footpaths and signposts, with visitor management on site, with the impacts of access on land management and with the constraints to access that deter significant numbers of people from making use of the countryside for recreation. The topic of constraints is one which has been less researched than most. Constraints may be overt, such as lack of transport, but there are also more subtle and less easily evaluated barriers, more perceptual in origin, such as fears of getting lost or feeling too lonely in the countryside. Thus the Lomond Hills project had a strong investigative flavour over a very wide field, albeit that some of the foregoing topics were only explored in a very prelimi- nary manner.

Examples of the work of the project are, a reconnaissance survey of the impacts of access onto land in the project area, an experimental recreational bus service (run under the whimsical promotional title of "Wee Mary-The Country Bus") mounted to explore to what extent it is possible to assist in the provision of transport to countryside recreation sites for populations with low levels of car ownership and a short exploratory study to examine the kind of constraints that influence those who do not visit countryside or do so infrequently. The latter study was contracted to the Tourism and Recreation Research Unit of Edinburgh University.

The fourth recreational project concerned with the countryside around towns was a

programme of <u>farm open days</u> providing opportunity for the public to visit working
farms near towns. The 23 farm open days averaged 1,000 visitors each. A com-
missioned research study of the educational value of such open days, mounted as part
of the project, confirmed that educational benefits do occur (Lee & Uzzell, 1980).
This project is at the stage of being transformed into a more permanent arrangement,
underthe wing of the Association of Agriculture with financial support from the
Commission.

Discussion

The preceding paragraphs provide brief sketches of four research and experimental
projects concerned with recreation in the countryside around towns. In some cases,
reports of the work are   already available; for others,written accounts will
appear in due course. In attempting to assemble a general picture of recreation
in the countryside around towns the same dilemma that exists in taking a synoptic
view of recreation elsewhere in countryside is encountered, namely that a reasonable amount is known about the use of managed recreation sites but little about
recreation dispersed outwith formal sites. The latter may be highly relevant
inasmuch as local neighbourhood recreation, originating at home and dispersed out
into the countryside may play an important role in recreation close to towns.
However, some generalities may be ventured from our existing knowledge.

In comparing the general findings of the survey work undertaken in parks in and
close to Glasgow with equivalent information gathered at rural recreation sites
distant from towns considerable contrasts are found. For example:-

- visitors to the city parks are drawn predominantly from a local catchment, with
a majority of visitors likely to be resident within two kilometres of the park;

- visitors to the city parks mainly comprise a regular clientelle with a majority
coming at least weekly for relatively short visits, and with small proportions of
first time visitors;

- at rural sites, the family group predominates but in the town parks individuals
are important in the profile of visiting groups;

- town park visits are much more evenly distributed through the week as compared
with the mainly weekend use of most rural sites (except where tourism is the main
generator of visits).

Of course, these generalisations need considerable qualification and it is not
strictly fair to polarise the nature of visits to town parks and those made to
rural sites. For example each recreation site will have its own profile of
visitors and patterns of visitation and activities according to the characteristics
of each site; thus town parks having resources appealing to a special market - such
as the art treasures of Pollok House and the future Burrell Gallery - will always
draw a proportion of visitors from some considerable distance. What is important
for this discussion is the proposition that most recreation sites close to towns
will have a strong urban flavour in drawing from a local catchment and in having -
in part - a neighbourhood park function, that is,serving as outlets for short
periods of recreation fitted into busy daily lives. A modest example of this occurs
in the survey of recreational use on the Union Canal which demonstrated that the
canal serves as a string of local neighbourhood parks for the communities through
which it passes, with 90% of towpath users being resident within a mile of the
canal.

Beyond the evidence gathered by site surveys, our knowledge about the distances
that people generally travel to their recreation destinations is very generalised

and comes mainly from home interview surveys, of which the principal Scottish
source is the Scottish Tourism and Recreation Survey (STARS) dating from 1973,
(which is being repeated in 1981 as the Scottish Leisure Survey). The evidence
on distance travelled for outdoor recreation is complex because distance is
closely related to the nature of the activity undertaken (TRRU, 1977). But for a
large number of recreation activities, active and passive, a majority of respon-
dents report return trip distances of less than 20 miles, implying, since more of
these journeys originate in towns, that the countryside close to towns is the
locus of much of this recreation, although some such trips will be to or within
towns. Participants in active sports (apart from distant resource based sports
like ski-ing and mountaineering) are very likely to have short trips and golf is
the obvious example to cite. On the other hand, for longer car-based day-trips it
is well known that the distribution of trip distance peaks at between 50 and 60
miles return trip, but in such journeys to more distant locations it is evident
that the journey itself is often an element of the recreational experience.

It has often been suggested that the countryside around towns has an important role
in holding visitors who might otherwise have penetrated out into more distant -
and it is implied - more vulnerable countryside. With our more abundant supply of
resources for recreation in proportion to population, this proposition is less
often heard in Scotland than in England. However, this sort of thinking is being
challenged at present (for example, Elson, 1979) on the grounds that the resources
of town edge recreation sites do not provide substitutes for the kinds of recreation
experience being sought at more distant locations. It is likely that attempts to
manipulate visitor flows by intercepting them close to towns represent over-sophis-
ticated recreation planning in that, in the absence of any coherent promotion of
informal recreation sites, the average recreationalist will not have knowledge of
the repertoire of sites to which it is hoped that he or she will divert.

Another virtue claimed for recreation provision in the countryside around towns
is proximity to the mass of the population. Accessibility is a vital issue in
countryside recreation provision. It is self-evident from the distribution of car
ownership and the substantial decline in route network and frequency of public
transport that significant proportions - often a majority - of residents in towns
do not have ready access to the sorts of provision being made for countryside
recreation, whether close to towns or in more distant countryside. One type of
response has been to create new recreational transport services and it was to
explore this aspect of access to countryside that an experimental bus service
(serving a catchment with very low car-ownership) was run as part of the Lomond
Hills Project. The service carried 674 passengers on eight Sundays in the summer
of 1980 and by comparison with other such experiments it did reasonably well
(CCS 1981b).

However, to run such a service is to come face to face with the realities of public
transport management, particularly that of setting fares at a level which the
customer will pay and finding the balance of cost from subsidy. There is considerable force in the argument that such revenue subsidy is wholly justified to match
the subsidy provided to the car-owner in the form of capital development to
accommodate car-based recreationalists. However, it is the case that even where
good public transport exists it is often little used. For example, at Pollok and
Rouken Glen parks no more than 10% of visitors used public transport, and at both
parks a majority came by car. Thus it may be that the lasting value of such
experimental bus services lies in the fact that they undoubtedly stimulate interest
in the need to explore possible methods of access to countryside for those without
their own transport.

It can be said that accessibility is all relative. Thus a park only a mile or so
distant may be just as inaccessible as one twenty-one miles away for those without

the means, the motivation or the information on how to get there. In that sense
it is necessary to look more critically at broad assertions that countryside around
towns is accessible countryside for town dwellers. Certainly it is closer and more
convenient but - except at the very edge of towns - it will not be more accessible
without intervention, particularly on behalf of those social groups who are
expected to benefit from provision close to towns. There is thus a need to continue
with inquiry into the range of constraints that affect those who do not visit countryside. Let it be clear that this is not to thrust countryside recreation on those
who have urban or home oriented leisure interests, but it is only proper to explore
and seek to understand the nature of concealed demand for access to countryside,
rather than assume from a distance that certain groups in society have no such
interest.

Discussion of access to countryside leads to the subject of the impact of access.
This is a difficult field. The Lomond Hills Project reconnaissance survey highlighted the extent to which the stress involved in maintaining constant vigilance
against adverse impacts may be as important a factor for farmers at the edge of
towns as the physical damage and loss incurred on the farm. However, this survey
area does not exemplify the worst range of problems found close to towns elsewhere
in Scotland and it is regrettable that, notwithstanding all the recent debate on
the urban fringe, there is no up-to-date and fine grained study of the impacts of
trespass onto land close to towns. That might not seem a very helpful comment to
those on the receiving end for whom solutions are required to problems that are
self-evident. Nonetheless, there is no evading the conclusion that many adverse
trespass impacts relate back to complex social problems affecting parts of our
towns and justify a deeper level of inquiry than has been undertaken hitherto.
Indeed, much of this kind of tresspass is not recreation in the positive sense of
that word, being often undirected play activity by young people which can quickly
develop into malicious or criminal behaviour. It would therefore be regrettable
if recreational access became a scapegoat for this wider range of difficult social
problems.

In concluding this short review there are two final points to be made. First, some
of the foregoing comment may seem to cut across the bows of current thinking about
recreation provision in the countryside around towns. If so, the intention is not
to draw away from the general importance of ensuring adequate provision for recreation close to towns - but to probe some attitudes that may be motivated by good
intention rather than realities. There are four particular areas where there is
likely to be continued emphasis on provision for recreation convenient to towns in
Scotland:

(i) to widen the existing range of opportunities for informal recreation in a
rural setting which will require attractive settings in mature lowland landscapes
or on the hill land that is convenient for most towns in the central belt of Scotland;

(ii) to remedy shortfall in provision in local open space where towns have expanded
outwards featuring sites that are genuinely accessible which are likely to be
found at the edge of towns;

(iii) to respond with management at locations where existing casual recreational
use requires effective supervision;

(iv) to provide opportunities for formal sports (which at present have an important
place in land-use close to towns) and which need to be convenient to participants,
but which cannot be accommodated within towns.

Beyond making new provision there may also be a need to ensure that existing
provision is adequately promoted and that such provision is relevant for present
needs.

Lastly, it is important to make a comment on the role of urban parks. The Commission has stressed in its main policy statement on outdoor recreation (CCS, 1974) that urban parks have a vital role in a system of parks extending out into countryside. The value of the surveys of parks in and near Glasgow has been to emphasise the importance of that role, indeed it is evident that the major city parks are receiving very substantial (six and even seven figure) numbers of visitors annually. Their importance lies largely in providing outlets for local neighbourhood use and as noted at the outset of this paper, it may be that this kind of informal recreation is more important in aggregate than the better researched day-trip to countryside. There may be,therefore,a need in some countryside at the edge of towns for more low key provision, appropriately managed for such use, rather than large, new, capital-intensive developments.

REFERENCES

Countryside Commission for Scotland (1974). A Park System for Scotland. The
    Commission, Perth.
Countryside Commission for Scotland (1981a). The Recreational Use of the Union
    Canal: A Reconnaissance Survey, Summer 1980. The Commission, Perth.
Countryside Commission for Scotland (1981b). Wee Mary The Country Bus: An Exper-
    iment in Transport to the Countryside for Recreation. The Commission, Perth.
Dartington Amenity Research Trust (1976). The Countryside Around Towns in Scotland.
    Unpublished report to the Countryside Commission for Scotland.
Elson, M.J. (1979). The Leisure Use of Green Belts. The Sports Council and Social
    Science Research Council, London.
Lee, T.R. and Uzzell, D.L. (1980). The Educational Effectiveness of the Farm Open
    Day. The Countryside Commission for Scotland, Perth.
Tourism and Recreation Research Unit (1977). STARS SERIES No. 5. Patterns of
    Outdoor Recreation in Scotland. TRRU Research Report 25, The Unit, University
    of Edinburgh.
Tourism and Recreation Research Unit (1978). Strathclyde Park, 1977: Monitoring
    the Use of a Country Park. TRUU Research Report 39, The Unit, University of
    Edinburgh.
Tourism and Recreation Research Unit (1980a).A Study of Four Parks in and around
    Glasgow: Report of Surveys Carried out in 1977 and 1978. TRUU Research Report
    44. The Unit, University of Edinburgh.
Tourism and Recreation Research Unit (1980b). Pollok Park, 1979: A Visitor Survey
    and Review of Management Implications. TRRU Research Report 45. The Unit,
    University of Edinburgh.

CHAPTER 4

DESCRIPTION AND COMMENT ARISING FROM A RECENT STUDY OF COUNTRYSIDE
AROUND THE MAJOR TOWNS IN CENTRAL REGION

Ken McDonald
Planning Department
Central Regional Council

ABSTRACT

The paper opens with a reminder to the audience of the landscape problems resulting from urban intrusion in the countryside around towns and goes on to describe
the content and findings of a study conducted by landscape consultants in Central
Region. The study was aimed at the identification of practical schemes for
securing landscape improvements. The paper considers one of the ideas suggested
by the consultants and uses the example of the Central Scotland Woodlands Project
to demonstrate the value of using a Project Officer as a means of instigating and
co-ordinating improvement works.

KEYWORDS

Urban intrusion in the countryside; a back garden for the town; landscape types;
"urban shadow"; project selection; positive management of land; Central Scotland
Woodlands Project; Open Land Action Plan; Project Officer.

INTRODUCTION

Landscape in the countryside around towns is the major issue considered in this
paper. Much of the content is a description of a study undertaken during 1979
by consultants sponsored jointly by the Countryside Commission for Scotland and
Central Regional Council. The Consultants were Anderson, Semens, Houston, Environmental Design Partnership and Cobham Resource Consultants working on behalf of
Brian Clouston and Partners.

It is not the purpose of this paper to be overly concerned with the name given to
the areas in question or to the outer boundaries, if such a thing exists in practice,
between peri-urban areas and countryside proper. There is a difference but perhaps
there is a decreasing amount of urban influence as one progresses from the town
rather than a definitive boundary. Everyone has subjective views on the significance of urban influence at different locations and these views are coloured by
the urban or rural emphasis of personal experience and background. People from a
city background may include in their perception an emphasis on positive scoring
for rural elements. People from rural backgrounds may place greater emphasis on
negative scoring for urban elements.

It may be appropriate to start with a brief picture as a reminder of the type of

of urban features which are developed in the countryside around towns and
diminish its character as countryside, both in relation to its appearance and its
function.

The area under discussion is used as a back garden for the town. Into it go town
extensions. Into it goes anything undesirable or too large for inclusion in the
urban fabric. One can expect to find there the fabric of essential services such
as power stations, sewage works and reservoirs; mental hospitals and burial grounds.
Scrap yards and noxious industries are a common feature. The area must be crossed
by roads and railways leading to the towns but also provides the shortest and most
convenient routes for bypasses. The back garden is also a convenient place to
extract minerals for the continued development of the towns. It is convenient for
the dumping of waste materials. Being the back garden, it is the obvious place to
play in, resulting in problems for the farmers associated with indiscriminate public
access. Large areas are also given over to formal sports and recreation. Many of
the built development may well be of good design but nevertheless they are urban.
Generally, the back garden is increasingly subjected to urban influence to the
detriment of its appearance as an area of countryside. Unfortunately, while it
functions as a back garden for the town, it also has to serve as the front garden
for visitors arriving from other places.

The names given to these areas around towns is not important. What is important is
to recognise that the open spaces between the urban features within these areas
each have an actual or potential value for providing town residents with a visual
or recreational experience of a countryside nature. The location in relation to
the town, the size, appearance, ownership and present use of each open area will
control the extent to which a countryside experience can be maintained, improved
or introduced and the extent to which it can be made available to the public.

BACKGROUND TO THE STUDY IN CENTRAL REGION

As a result of discussions instigated by the Countryside Commission for Scotland
about the Dartington Amenity Research Trust Report (DART 1976), Central Regional
Council agreed to participate in the funding and management of a study of the
countryside around towns in Central Region.

The Regional Council had three reasons for welcoming the opportunity to have a
study carried out; firstly, it could lead to the achievement of improvements in
the area; secondly, the specialists to be employed had expertise which was not
available within the staff resources of the Council; thirdly, the appointment of
consultants would ensure a much greater commitment of time to the consideration of
the issues than Council staff could give. Similar motives also resulted in the
Regional Council participating in the Central Scotland Woodlands Project to which
reference will be made later.

It was decided to appoint consultants to undertake the study over a period of one
year. A brief was prepared by officials from the Countryside Commission and the
Regional Council. It laid particular stress on consideration of landscape problems
and the identification of practical schemes for improvement. It did, however, recognise the need to have regard to the other main issues of land use and recreation.
The identification of opportunities for improvement on these fronts was also called
for but emphasis had to be placed on the appearance of the area. Particular stress
was given to the image of the area as seen by people passing through it. Image
building is important to local and national authorities in relation to the attrac-
tion of industry and tourists. In practice, throughout the study equal consideration was given to the needs of residents.

A steering Committee of Officers from the Countryside Commission and Central Region was set up to advise the consultants and to monitor their progress. Representatives from the three District Council Planning Departments were also invited to participate, i.e. Falkirk, Stirling and Clackmannan.

The drawing of the boundary of the study area was influenced by a variety of local factors but set out to embrace all of the major towns in Central Region including Falkirk, Grangemouth, Stirling and Alloa (Fig. 4.1). The boundary was drawn with recognition of geographical differences which exist between the study area and adjoining areas e.g. the lowland and the upland at Falkirk and Denny, the remarkably sharp division between the town and the country to the west of Stirling, the distinction between the central area of Clackmannan and the valley of the River Devon along the foot of the Ochil Hills. Perhaps as much regard was given to the resources available, limitations imposed by the Regional boundary and the political expediency of including a part of each District. The line was not drawn with any precision and the Consultants were advised to regard it as flexible when considering detailed local issues. The urban areas within the study area were excluded from the Consultant's remit by reference to the inclusion of only 'designated countryside', i.e. as identified in map form by the Secretary of State in accordance with the Countryside (Scotland) Act, 1967. Again, the Consultants were advised not to be unduly concerned by the detail of the drawn boundary.

DESCRIPTION OF THE STUDY

The Consultants' final report was completed last summer (1980) and is presently the subject of consultation with the main agencies who have an interest in the area. It is hoped that the consultations will reveal a general level of support which is sufficient to confirm the justification for certain of the major proposals to be taken forward to the stage of implementation.

The Consultants' report is divided into three main parts:-

1) Surveys of landscape, recreation and productive rural land uses to identify problems.

2) An identification and assessment of projects.

3) Detailed discussion of four projects which were selected for closer investigation.

Landscape

Because of the emphasis placed by the sponsors on the identification of practical schemes for improvement, the brief specifically restricted the amount of time to be spent on the survey stage. The Consultants had to demonstrate a thorough understanding of the issues involved but were not in a position to adopt exhaustive specialised techniques when examining the area. When considering the study area, the Consultants identified a broad classification of five landscape types but stressed that this was used simply as a tool for them to acquaint themselves with the area and not to represent a formal classification of type and quality. The types identified are as follows (Fig. 4.2):-

(i) The flat low-lying countryside adjacent to the Forth which has few hedges and woodland but an extensive network of electricity lines.

(ii) The lowland inland from the carseland (i.e. as in (i) above) which has a greater number of landscape features and is more interesting.

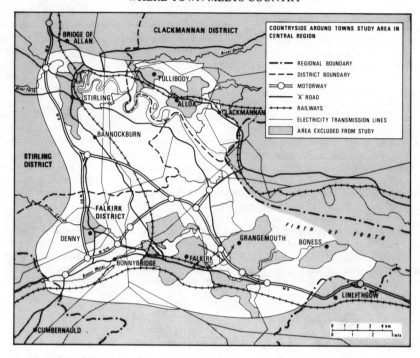

Fig. 4.1   COUNTRYSIDE AROUND TOWNS STUDY AREA IN CENTRAL REGION

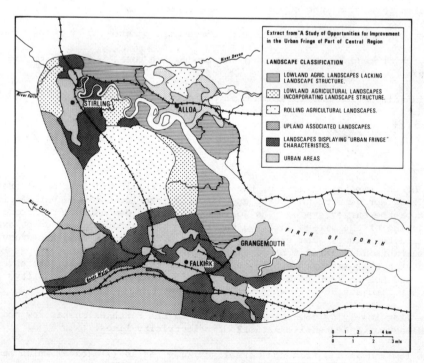

Fig. 4.2   LANDSCAPE CLASSIFICATION

(iii) The rolling agricultural landscape with a mixture of arable and pasture with well-defined field boundaries but marred by the exposed edge of settlements, large-scale industry and mineral extraction.

(iv)   The upland landscape which is exposed, mainly used for grazing and suffers from the evidence of former and active industries such as brick-making, quarrying and mining.

(v)   Landscape with urban fringe characteristics around the main settlements.

Despite the fact that the Consultants found evidence of urban influence in all of the landscape zones within the study area, they were able to identify certain areas which could be distinguished from the rest by their notable urban fringe character-istics. The Consultants made use of the phrase "urban shadow" when considering these fringe areas and concluded that they represented perhaps 40% of the study area.

The primary factors creating landscape problems throughout the study area were identified as:-

- Urban intrusion into the countryside.

- Derelict and degraded land associated with former and existing industrial activity or awaiting new developments.

- Poorly considered landscape design in relation to some development sites.

- Limited management of landscape features, probably reflecting economic constraints on landowners.

- The unauthorised dumping of litter and refuse.

- Severance of the land by an increasing road network and its impact on the land-scape.

Recreation

The brief made it necessary for the Consultants to give more limited consideration to recreation. However, they identified an absence of formal or informal access areas and noted the existence of poorly signposted footpaths. They concluded that many people were going outwith the area for recreational opportunities but noted that the lack of provision was leading to the use of private farmland and woodland for recreation. They consulted farming interests in the study area and found evidence of conflict as a result although concluded that it was at an acceptable level.

Land Use

Their consideration of productive rural land uses identified a range of problems being faced by the farmers and foresters including severance and fragmentation of land, the loss of land to urban development, uncertainty about the future, public intrusion and atmospheric pollution.

These problems have resulted in the sub-optimal use and abandonment of land, increased costs, limitations on the type of farming which could be undertaken and the removal of woodlands from dedication agreements. The Consultants considered it important to maintain urban fringe land in genuine agricultural use both because of its value as an irreplaceable resource and because of its appearance.

Project Selection

The Consultants prepared a sizeable list of specific 'spot' and area projects each of which would contribute in some way to the resolution of actual problems identified in the Central Region study area. The brief called for detailed consideration to be given to a selected sample of projects. The comprehensive list was sifted through by the Consultants and the Steering Committee using a range of criteria (Fig. 4.3). Perhaps the most significant factor which contributed to the process was the desire to identify projects which would be innovative and perhaps be relevant for other situations outwith Central Region.

Almost all of the projects are considered worthwhile and worthy of pursuit when resources are available. Some of the smaller scale schemes have already resulted in allocations being made from existing budgets for tree planting around the edge of settlements.

Selected Projects

Four projects were selected for further investigation by the Consultants in the final part of their study:

(a) An Open Land Action Plan for one of the urban fringe or"shadow"areas which they identified. They considered that a plan would form the basis of a comprehensive approach to urban fringe problems balancing the planning and management of land use, landscape and recreation.

(b) A Farm Landscape Project aimed to demonstrate the ways in which the differing objectives of modern commercial farming, landscape and wild life conservation, sport and recreation can be reconciled on individual farms.

(c) Callendar Wood Access Agreement which would seek to regularise public access to this commercial woodland adjacent to Falkirk in an attempt to resolve the present conflict between the unauthorised access and the woodland management objectives of the owner.

(d) Stirling Eastern Distributor Road - the Consultants outlined the investigations which they consider necessary to identify opportunities for integrating this new road into the landscape and improving the eventual view from it.

The Farm Landscapes Project and the Roads Landscape Issue are relevant to the countryside around towns but are equally applicable in the countryside generally. The Woodlands Access Agreement deals with only one of the problems which arise in the countryside around towns. Of the four projects, the Open Land Action Plan is the most worthy of further consideration in this paper because it is directed at the whole range of fundamental problems. Of the 7 fringe areas defined by the Consultants, the Banknock/Bonnybridge area was selected for the preparation of a plan because of the high incidence of problems in that area.

The Banknock/Bonnybridge Plan

The Consultants believe that one of the central problems in these fringe areas is the lack of positive management of significant areas of land and that this non or poor use of land results in a confused and unattractive landscape. The plan for the Banknock/Bonnybridge area aims primarily at landscape improvement but recognises the need for amalgamation and restructuring of farming units to counter the management difficulties which have resulted from fragmentation caused by urban and transport developments. The plan contains proposals for rationalised field boundaries, reinstatement of walls and fences, tree planting, clearance of

Extract from "A Study of Opportunities for Improvement in the Urban Fringe of Part of Central Region"

SELECTION CRITERIA

Legend: ○ Significant   ● Very Significant

SELECTION CRITERIA	STIRLING BANNOCK-BURN PLEAN	COWIE-PLEAN	ALLOA FRINGES	BANKNOCK BONNY-BRIDGE	MID CARRON VALLEY	FALKIRK GRANGE-MOUTH GREEN BELT	GLEN VILLAGE-POLMONT MADDISTON
ESSENTIAL STUDY DIMENSIONS							
1 Areas requiring comprehensive treatment	○	○		●	●	●	●
2 Opportunities for a variety of improvement methods	●	○	●	●	●	●	●
3 Opportunities for innovation	○	○	○	●	●	●	●
4 Practicability	●	●		●	○		
5 Opportunities for a corporate approach		●		●	●	●	○
6 Opportunities for community involvement	●	○	○	○	●	●	●
LANDSCAPE PROBLEMS							
7 Lack of coherent visual structure	●	○		●	○		●
8 Urban intrusion	●	○	○	●	●	●	●
9 Lack of landscape management	○	○	●	○		○	●
10 Limited aims of landowners		●		○	●	○	○
11 Derelection and degradation	○	○		●	●	○	○
12 Dumping and litter	○	○	○	○	○	○	○
13 Poor image	●	○	○	●	●	●	○
14 Visually deficient corridors	○		○	●			
RECREATIONAL POTENTIAL							
15 Derelict and degraded land	○	○		●	●	○	○
16 Footpaths	○			○	○		○
17 Attractive areas		○					
18 Historic places of interest	○				○		○
19 Wildlife values	○		○				○
PRODUCTIVE LAND USE PROBLEMS							
20 Severance and fragmentation		○		●	○	●	●
21 Large areas requiring restoration	○	○		○	●	○	
22 Land awaiting development		○					
23 Vandalism in woodlands			○		●		●
24 Disturbance to agriculture		○	●	○	○		○
25 Business uncertainty	○		○			●	●
ACCEPTABILITY CRITERIA							
26 Sponsor/District Commitment	○	○		○	○	○	○
27 Incidence of public land ownership	●	●	○		○	○	
28 Benefits to residents	○	○	○	●	●	○	●
29 Benefits to visitors	○			○	●		
30 Demonstrability	○	●	○	●	●	●	○
31 Applicability	○	●	●	●	○	●	●
32 Environmental improvement already started	○	●	●		●	●	○
			○				○

Fig. 4.3 SELECTION CRITERIA

derelict land etc. The detail is not important; the concept of a comprehensive
approach is the vital issue. A comprehensive plan provides a target to be sought
after as resources become available.

Of even greater importance is the process to be adopted for implementation of such
a plan. No single agency has been given or has taken the remit to prepare such
plans which deal with rural land use, landscape management and recreational access.
Each agency operates within more narrowly defined remits and is unable to deal
with the issues in a comprehensive manner. Given that a plan is prepared, there
is no direct means of providing for its implementation since there is no legislative framework to ensure that changes in rural land uses correspond with the plan
or to ensure that desirable changes are made to happen. This should be read as a
statement of fact and not as an ambition on the part of the planning profession.

Implementation is therefore dependent on persuasion, co-operation and encouragement. In recognising this, the Consultants recommended that a project officer be
employed by the Local Authorities to pursue the implementation of the plan. The
project officer would establish links with the agencies, landowners and property
owners and would seek out ways in which the proposals could be undertaken either
using existing sources of funds or failing this, by means of additional inputs
from the Local Authorities.

There can be no doubt that the process of communication and persuasion is likely
to lead to solutions and improvements which are more generally acceptable to all
of the parties involved than would be the case if legislation was introduced to
increase the controls and restrictions. However, achievement through influence
calls for commitment from the public authorities. There must be recognition of
the problem by the politicians and a willingness to commit resources, particularly
staff, to the work. Gaining recognition of the problem is not a real difficulty.
The difficulty comes when the problem is considered in the context of the other
responsibilities of the public authorities. There are so many social issues which
have to take priority. The current economic recession creates worsening problems
and reduces the resources available to deal with them.

The Central Scotland Woodlands Project

The Central Scotland Woodlands Project (Fig. 4.4) referred to earlier, is an
example of a project which has political support. It was set up two years ago as
an experiment aimed primarily at the achievement of landscape improvements in a
bleak upland area in south Central Scotland. This is an area of depressed and
marginal agriculture and poor environment, blighted by the relics of past industrial
activity and mineral working. The aims of the project are comprehensive including
land use, recreation and wild life objectives, but considerable emphasis has been
placed on the appearance of the area and, for this purpose, increasing the amount
of tree cover is seen as a primary means by the authorities involved. The project
is jointly sponsored by the Countryside Commission for Scotland, Strathclyde,
Lothian and Central Regional Councils.

Pursuit of the objectives is by means of a Project Officer and an Assistant Project
Officer whose job it is to identify opportunities for tree planting by approaching
the various users of land in the area and encouraging, advising and assisting them
to undertake the schemes. The Project Officers also maintain links with the public
and private agencies who have an interest in the area or a contribution to make,
including the Department of Agriculture and Fisheries for Scotland, the Forestry
Commission, the Scottish Development Agency, the Land and Woodland Owners Associ-
ations, the National Farmers Union and the Local Authorities.

By the end of the first year, sufficient sites had been identified to accommodate

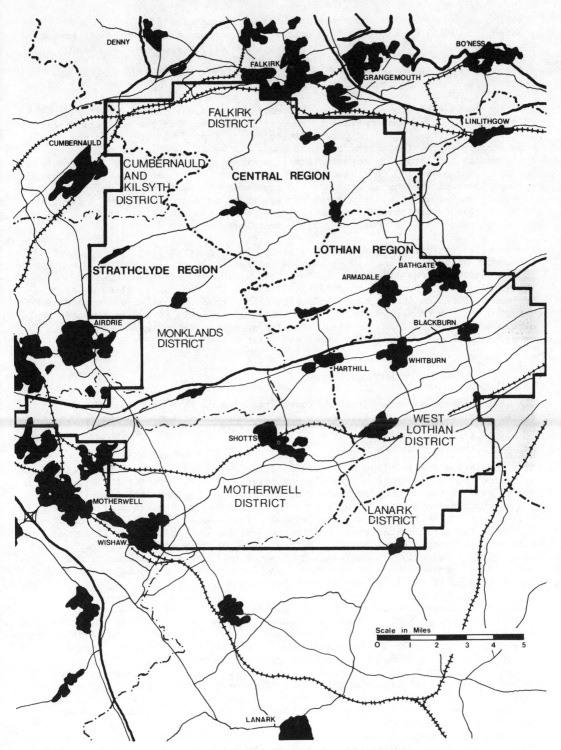

Fig. 4.4   CENTRAL SCOTLAND WOODLANDS PROJECT AREA

planting in excess of 750,000 trees of which approximately 365,000 have been
planted (May 1981) on a total of 97 sites. Every opportunity is taken to encourage the involvement of local communities, particularly through the schools.
Particular attention is now being given to planting schemes around settlements in
order to improve their appearance and in many instances to provide shelter in
otherwise exposed locations.

The project is achieving results and is proving successful. Much credit must go
to the many agencies who continue to support the project but the most significant
factor must be the skills and personalities of the Project Officers and the
considerable initiative which they have shown. They are willing to act as cata-
lysts and co-ordinators in any situation, large or small, which they consider has
potential for advancing the objectives of the project. In each situation, they
explore the various sources of funds and assistance to seek ways in which to
implement improvements. The project employs existing sources and levels of grant.
They experiment with simplified contract procedures and planting techniques to
encourage landowners to undertake improvement works.

The detailed workings of the project will not be considered here. The concept is
the important element since it broadly demonstrates the type of approach which the
Consultants were suggesting for the Open Land Action Plan in the Banknock/
Bonnybridge area. The primary difference is that the Central Scotland Woodlands
Project operates on an "opportunist" basis rather than on a planned approach as
intended for the Open Land Action Plan. This mainly reflects a difference in scale
although the Open Land Action Plan calls for much more intensive consideration to
be given to all of the problems which may exist in an area.

DISCUSSION AND CONCLUSIONS

The definition of an area serves to focus attention on it. The appointment of a
Project Officer with a specific remit to pursue the objectives produces results
because of the unhindered attention that the officer can give the job.

Making staff available on this basis requires political commitments. The Countryside Commission for Scotland has encouraged the commitment of Local Authorities
by taking the lion's share of the cost associated with Project Officer Experiments.
In the case of the Central Scotland Woodland Project, the Regional Councils have
agreed to it being continued for a further three years on the basis of the commission's share being progressively reduced. This demonstrates recognition of the
fact that the experimental period of the project is passing and that it is becoming
more akin to a service which should be the responsibility of the local authorities
in the area. Recently, at the request of Motherwell and West Lothian District
Councils the project has been extended. The demonstration given by the project has
led to this political interest and commitment.

Political commitment can also come from public concern. Public concern can only
come from increased awareness of the problem. Awareness in turn can only come from
education. This is generally a slow process and one which definitely needs infinite
patience. The process of change and deterioration in the countryside around towns
is not sufficiently dramatic in scale or speed to become widely recognised as a
matter for concern by local communities, without it being drawn to their attention
by concerned agencies like the Countryside Commission for Scotland and the local
authorities. Action by all the concerned public agencies will continue to be
required in advance of wide public awareness and concern. Nevertheless, when
public awareness can be increased, for example by the efforts of Project Officers
and Countryside Ranger Services, voluntary action by communities could become a
much more common and significant element in the creation of landscape improvements

and the reduction of conflicts with land users in the fringe areas.

REFERENCES

Anderson, Semens, Houston. Environmental Design Partnership and Cobham Resource
     Consultants on behalf of Brian Clouston and Partners (1980). A Study of
     Opportunities for Improvement in the Urban Fringe of Part of Central Region
     with Special Reference to Landscape and Land Use. Unpublished report to the
     Countryside Commission for Scotland and Central Regional Council.
Countryside Commission for Scotland (1980). Central Scotland Woodlands Project:
     First Interim Report, February 1979-January 1980. The Commission, Perth.
Countryside Commission for Scotland (1981). Central Scotland Woodlands Project:
     Second Interim Report, February 1980-January 1981. The Commission, Perth.
Dartington Amenity Research Trust (1976). The Countryside Around Towns in Scotland.
     Unpublished report to the Countryside Commission for Scotland.
Lothian Regional Council (1978). Central Scotland Woodlands Project. Department
     of Physical Planning, Lothian Regional Council, Edinburgh.

COMMENT ON CHAPTERS 2, 3 and 4 BY SYMPOSIUM DISCUSSANT

George Gordon
University of Strathclyde

Peri-urban areas can be examined from many viewpoints. Sometimes these stand-
points appear to be in direct opposition such as the urban-rural dichotomy.
However, if peri-urban areas are characterised by a multiplicity of different
activities it is perhaps inevitable that stresses and strains will exist in the
land use system of these areas and that discord may occur between certain activities in terms of environmental impact.

These three papers are linked by the activities and initiatives of the Countryside
Commission and, to a considerable extent, by the DART report. It is important to
remember that the DART group were given a specific task, to report on the potential
of the countryside around towns with particular regard for environmental conservation and informal outdoor recreation. Thus the papers adopted a very particular
view of the nature, problems and purpose of peri-urban areas. If there is a
spatial coincidence between the types of areas within the remit of the DART study
and peri-urban areas then one can seriously question the geographical assumptions
implicit in the terms of reference of that study, notably the idea that peri-urban
areas are, in effect, solely or primarily areas of countryside.

Peri-urban areas are generally recognised as zones of competition between very
varied land uses. They have also been described as zones of transition. The
latter definition involves the belief that, in a comparatively short period of
time, these areas will become part of the expanding urban or metropolitan area.
Mr. McDonald illustrates that dimension when he mentions areas lying in the shadow
of urban settlements. However only 40% of the Central Region study area is classed
as urban shadow. Does that imply that the majority of the study area is of
marginal relevance to the topic under discussion?

The anology between back gardens and peri-urban areas, in terms of function and
environmental planning, is certainly interesting. But the exact boundaries of a
back garden are normally known and the responsibility for its maintenance is clearly
vested in a readily identified person, normally the occupant of the property. Mr.
Huxley illustrated the practical merits of a spatial definition of peri-urban areas
although one might suggest that the physical dimensions should relate to the size
of the urban centre, the density of the urban settlement pattern and other factors
such as topography and agricultural productivity. It would also seem desirable to
have a carefully articulated planning strategy for peri-urban areas which recognised
and accommodated the nature of the area. There was perhaps an implication in Mr.
McDonald's paper that peri-urban areas were being returned to countryside. Of

40

course environmental improvement should be a fundamental component of policy for these areas but incursions of urban land use will continue.   Indeed one of the most noticeable recent changes in the Banknock-Bonnybridge area has been the construction of a substantial area of industrial premises in the form of bonded warehouses.

This is not to advocate the rape of the countryside but rather to suggest that it is necessary to ask some fundamental questions about peri-urban areas in terms of the best use of that particular geographical resource.   Need it simply be a zone of conflict between urban areas and countryside?   Mr. Mackay warned that some attitudes about the use of peri-urban areas for urban-oriented informal recreation space might be motivated by good intention rather than realities.   Should there be more emphasis on the provision of playing fields both at peri-urban locations and perhaps even more pertinently in inner city locations?

It is possible to have a neat and productive back garden.   The notion that peri-urban areas should become the front garden for the traveller or visitor conjures up pictures of the front room which remained exclusively for use on special occasions.   The speakers from the Countryside Commission rightly suggested that there should be research into the validity of present policy relating to recreation in peri-urban areas.   Ideally it should be part of an open-minded extensive study of the nature and problems of peri-urban areas and of the roles of such areas in our society.

CHAPTER 5
THE SCOTTISH DEVELOPMENT AGENCY ROLE IN ENVIRONMENTAL IMPROVEMENT
AND RENEWAL OF DERELICT LAND ON THE URBAN FRINGE.

R.J. Bleasdale
Scottish Development Agency

ABSTRACT

The paper examines the role of the Agency in environmental improvement and names
some completed and current schemes in peri-urban areas of Scotland.

KEYWORDS

Scottish Development Agency; environmental improvement; derelict land;
urban fringe; DART Report of 1976.

The Scottish Development Agency was founded in December 1975, at which time it
absorbed the Scottish Industrial Estates Corporation, the Small Industries Council
for Rural Areas and took over work previously done - albeit in a different manner -
by the Derelict Land Unit of the SDD. The Agency's overall remit is defined in
the SDA Act of 1975 as being to further economic development, to safeguard employment and to improve the environment. It has wide powers of investment and a major
role in factory building and estate development, being Scotland's largest industrial landlord.

Its other major role is in environmental improvement and the renewal of derelict
land, and the question is sometimes posed as to whether there is a conflict of
interests in an organisation charged simultaneously with industrial expansion and
environmental improvement. Certainly the industrial revolution created physical
devastation the scars of which are still with us and during this century too there
has been much industrial development which paid little regard for its surroundings
and its impact upon them. However, the Agency sees no conflict in its twin role.
Indeed, it is one of its great potential strengths that for the first time these
have been combined in one single organisation. The official definition of derelict
land is "land so damaged by past industrial or other development that it is incapable of beneficial use without treatment"; a definition broad enough to
encompass a very great range of areas without setting limits to size, either at
the top or the bottom of the range.

No one has a specific figure for the amount of derelict land in Scotland. An
inspired guess has been made at 45,000 acres but in any case the numbers are not
important and change every day.

However, it is clear that much of this dereliction is within, or adjacent to, urban areas and most of the Agency's land renewal work has been done in such locations, with a few spectacular exceptions.

Budgets are limited and the Agency cannot assume the responsibilities and obligations of other statutory bodies. However, it is often possible to work in close co-operation with others and thereby achieve total results which would otherwise be unattainable. For instance, many Local Authority inspired projects involve them in finishing works following the completion of the basic schemes by the Agency, such as the provision of hard playing services and games equipment on recovered and landscaped sites. There exists an excellent relationship with the Tourist Board - and many projects have a tourism orientated objective - the Countryside Commission, the Highlands and Islands Development Board, Local Authorities and other bodies.

Schemes have included the treatment of gap sites, rebuilding of walls and fences, the cleaning of rivers and canals and the total clearance of past industrial or other establishments such as mine-workings, brickworks, railway stations, disused factories and other buildings. They include provision of extensive walkways, and the reclamation of large tracts of land for industry, housing, leisure activities and public open space. The Agency strongly supports realistic and discriminating conservation and although its priorities are with clearance and redevelopment there are a number of ways in which it can play a positive part, including the modernisation and re-use of older buildings, conservation projects where there is joint involvement with the Tourist Board; and those connected with the craft industries, some of which are conservation orientated. Other environmental schemes incorporate areas within which the conservation of wild life has been maintained or encouraged.

The right location for factories and estates is of prime importance in attracting new industry and in this context the greenfield site still has a place in strategic planning. In most cases this implies a location on the perimeter of an urban area and the impact of such development needs very careful consideration as it can be devastating unless handled with care. However, it is possible to minimise the adverse effects whilst taking advantage of the obvious benefits.

Where the urban boundary is confused it may be possible to integrate new industrial development with built-up areas whilst landscaping and planting in such a way as to soften outlines and merge with the more rural background. Where an estate has to intrude directly into rural land the problem is more difficult to handle and the maximum benefit needs to be sought from existing planting and other natural features.

Many land renewal projects have been carried out on the urban fringe and in some cases this has resulted in an extension of the town - for instance where there has been an industrial or commercial afteruse. In others the effect has been to extend the rural area or rural and recreational facilities. The DART Report of 1976 presented a clear and interesting statement regarding the countryside around towns, the potential and the philosophy of its use. It assisted the Agency in formulating policy on certain types of environmental schemes and it is hoped that a contribution can be made towards some of the experimental work recommended.

COMPLETED AND CURRENT SCHEMES

At the Devon Colliery on the outskirts of Alloa, over one million tons of tip material was removed and placed in the lower wetland in the flood plain of the River Devon. About 140 acres of land has been returned to general grazing with some tree shelter belts introduced to blend the reclaimed site into the surrounding countryside.

The Gore and Emily bings on the A7 at Newtongrange have been regraded and as well
as providing much needed playing fields in the area, some 10 acres of land has
been made available for light industry. Extensive areas have been planted along-
side the A7, and a picnic area has also been included. A worked out bing at
Balnardie on the north west edge of Bathgate incorporates football pitches and a
major event area, as well as making provision for a future nine hole golf course.

The Auchinstarry quarry scheme on the south edge of Kilsyth, which incidentally
won an American Landscape Award, incorporates many interesting and novel uses.
The quarry was water filled but has now been shallowed to make an excellent boating
pond, picnic and passive recreation facilities provided, and the rock face checked
and cleared for use by rock climbers. In Glasgow, five major park schemes have
now been completed and one of these, Auchinlea Park, on the outskirts of Easterhouse,
now boasts a nine hole golf course, 3 football pitches and a more formal garden
area with a fairly large pond. Before restoration this area had within it a small
coal tip, a quarry and a large area of wetland but had been for many years used as
a general tip area by the City of Glasgow. It now provides a much needed recreational area for the whole of Easterhouse. Dereliction exists the length and
breadth of the country. Many of our rivers as they flow through our towns have
suffered from pollution, and now dereliction, since industry tended to settle along
the banks using the water for either cooling purposes or power. By clearing such
dereliction, linear parks and walkway systems have been provided, and one of the
best examples which is now virtually complete is the Kelvin Walkway in Glasgow.
This provides a link from the countryside at Killermont to the city centre.

REFERENCE

Dartington Amenity Research Trust (1976). The Countryside Around Towns in Scotland.
    Unpublished report to the Countryside Commission for Scotland.

THE SCOTTISH DEVELOPMENT AGENCY: TWO EXAMPLES OF DERELICT
LAND RECLAMATION SCHEMES.

A.R. Gilchrist
Scottish Development Agency

ABSTRACT

The paper details land reclamation projects which have been completed at two former
sites of extractive industry, Auchinstarry Quarry, Kilsyth and Devon Colliery,
Alloa.

KEYWORDS

Reclamation; multiple recreational uses; urban fringe; agricultural afteruse;
tree planting.

AUCHINSTARRY QUARRY, KILSYTH

Extensive quarrying of whinstone has been carried out over many years on the
southern fringe of Kilsyth. This whinstone dyke forms a 40 m high ridge between
the town and the River Kelvin, and quarrying was carried out from the south side.
There was little excavation below general ground level and when quarrying finished
in the early 1960's, a shallow water filled basin and a 40 m high rock cliff face

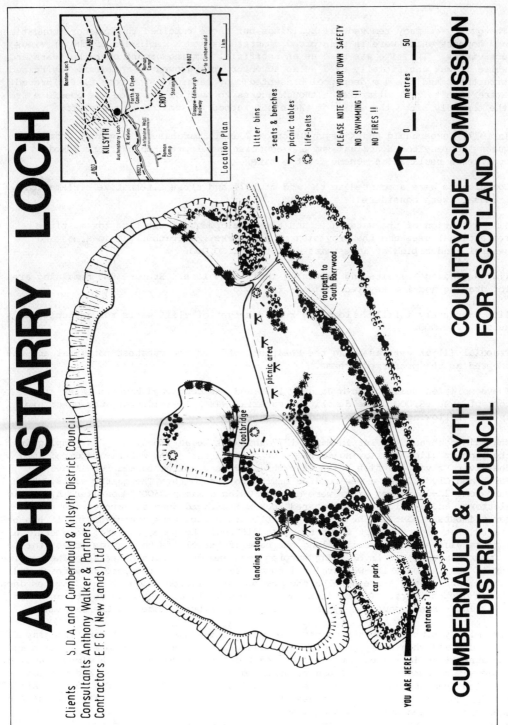

Fig. 5.1 AUCHINSTARRY LOCH

remained (Fig. 5.1).

The quarry company removed all buildings but there remained the crusher foundations
and hoppers which were in reinforced concrete as stark reminders of the previous
activities. The site was used as an unofficial dumping ground over the years and
while it was unofficially used as an adventure playground by children, the ruined
structures and the 4 m deep pool presented many hazards. The rock cliffs proved
attractive to rock climbers, although access to much of the face was possible from
the top only since the water of the basin lapped the bottom of the cliff.

In 1977, Cumbernauld and Kilsyth District Council purchased the quarry from the
quarry company for a nominal sum and Scottish Development Agency were asked to
consider a reclamation scheme for the site.

Consultants were appointed at the end of 1977 and three alternative reclamation
proposals were considered:-

(i)   Retention of the water area and the development of the site for multiple
recreational uses and the provision of car parks, footpaths, picnic areas and
general landscaping at an estimated cost of £100,000.

(ii) Regrading the site and partially infill the loch. Prepare the remaining area
for grazing and low key recreation - £115,000.

(iii) Completely infill the loch and reduce height of cliff walls for agricultural
uses - £250,000.

Proposal (i) as well as being the cheapest, offered the greatest potential and was
adopted as the preferred scheme.

The demolition phase began in January 1979 and was completed 8 weeks later at a
cost of some £9,000. The demolition material was laid aside for subsequent use
in the shallowing of the loch and landscape works.

The main contract was let in March 1979 and work began immediately in pumping dry
the loch to allow shallowing works to be carried out. The water was pumped into
the River Kelvin and fish which were stranded were collected and put into the
Forth and Clyde Canal a few hundred metres to the south. The quarry walls, which
were some 20-35 metres high, were checked using a Simon S300 "Moonraker" hydraulic
platform, and all loose or weathered rock was cleaned down to improve the faces
for climbers. Most of the earlier established climbs were preserved and it has been
stated that some are just about the most difficult to be encountered anywhere. A
2 metre wide shelf was built along the base of the cliffs to provide access for
climbers above water level using surplus rock and demolition material. The remainder of surplus material was graded into the basin to form the core of a beach and
give a safe gentle slope down to the new bed of the loch which is now 3 metres deep
at its deepest part. To add interest, the peninsula was cut away at its neck and
an island formed connected by an 18 metre long timber bridge to the mainland.

Preliminary site investigation revealed substantial quantities of sand and gravel,
whin dust and whin scalpings. The sand and gravel were used to form the beach and
the other materials used for car park and footpath construction. A timber landing
stage was constructed to allow development of boating and canoeing, and the loch
refilled from the adjacent River Kelvin and restocked with fish (Fig. 5.1). All
soil on the site was graded and used for the grassed areas of the site without the
need for imported material, and areas planted to integrate the area into the
surrounding attractive landscape. Indigenous species in areas of the site include
alder, ash, oak, hawthorn, rowan, birch and willow, and smaller areas associated

with the site features, have been planted with mixes of hazel, blackthorn, dogrose, elder, dogwood, broom and snowberry. Several specimen willows and pines are planted on the banks of the loch.

It is intended that the island, the hill and the field to the south of the track, have little or no maintenance to enable wild flowers and broom to naturalise. Other grass areas will also be allowed to grow with only minimal maintenance to enable a more natural meadowland to develop. Picnic tables, benches and litter bins have been provided with funds made available by the Countryside Commission for Scotland. In the interest of safety, a security fence has been built a few metres back from the top of the rock face to separate the park from the adjoining housing development. The park has a southern aspect and provides facilities for rock climbing, boating, canoeing, bathing, nature study, fishing and picnicking. It is also within a few hundred metres of the Forth and Clyde Canal where potential exists for longer distance boating or walking.

The park is an excellent example of an urban fringe reclamation scheme, and has been recognised internationally in winning the Judges Award from the American Landscape Contractors Association in 1980. The total cost of the project funded by Scottish Development Agency was £153,800 which for a 5.7 ha site represents a unit cost of £2.70 per square metre.

DEVON COLLIERY, ALLOA

Coal was first worked in pre-Reformation days in shallow seams near the surface but with the passage of years, these shallow workings became deep pits.

The first pit was sunk near Alloa in 1519 but it was not until about 1835 that extensive coal working began in the area. The Devon Colliery was the Alloa Coal Company's main pit, however water presented a major problem and forced the closure of the pit in 1854. It was re-opened in 1881 and the shaft deepened, with new hydraulic pumps being installed to deal with the water. 1922 saw a significant change at Devon with the introduction of electrical power, and in 1937 a central electricity generating plant was installed at Devon to supply power to all the Company's undertakings. In 1931 the first pithead baths were opened combined with locker and boot rooms and catering for over 600 men. A canteen was opened in 1942 and the colliery finally closed in 1959.

The site was purchased in 1977 by Central Regional Council and proposals for reclamation were prepared.

The site occupies a prominent position on the hillside overlooking the Devon Valley. The proposals were that most of the area should be returned to an agricultural after-use but that the Beam Engine House should be retained and would act as a focal point for a small picnic area from which there would be excellent views to the Ochil Hills and the Devon Valley. Sufficient tree planting would be included to blend the scheme into the existing landscape. The main reclamation scheme presented four distinct problems. These were: 2 pit shafts, the large 70m high tip on the hillside, the slurry ponds containing over 80,000 tons of slurry at the toe of the tip, and three areas of wet-land covering some 1.45 ha in the bends of the River Devon. (Fig. 5:2).

The shafts were located in the area to be used for the future picnic site and while the shafts had been filled in 1963 shortly after the time of closure of the pit, it was decided to ensure their future safety by capping. A 600mm thick reinforced concrete slab was cast over the 6m diameter shafts and backfilled to ground level.

Fig. 5.2   DEVON COLLIERY—BEFORE RECLAMATION

Fig. 5.3   DEVON COLLIERY—AFTER RECLAMATION

The National Coal Board were able to remove over 80,000 tons of the usable slurry before the main earthworks contract was let and as well as making available an energy resource, it reduced the quantities of material to be moved on the site.

Since it was intended to return much of the site to agriculture there was a need to obtain as much soil from the site as possible. The scheme finally carried out, involved draining the three ponds and extracting silt and sub soil from these areas. The material was stacked for re-use on the latter stages of the scheme.

Virtually the whole of the main bing, some $600,000m^3$, was removed into the slurry pond and wet-land areas at the bottom of the hill, raising the ground level in this area by about 2m. The previously excavated soils were then re-spread over the whole reclaimed area giving a minimum depth of soil of about 100mm. In all, some 38 ha were returned to an agricultural use and some 5 ha planted out as shelter belts. The scheme as designed has endeavoured to produce field patterns which are similar to the surrounding countryside. In fact one of the features of a scheme of this nature is that after a few years the old scars will have healed and the area will almost be indistinguishable from the adjacent areas. (Fig.5:3).

The project began in October 1977 and was completed in the autumn of 1978. Some light grazing was permitted in 1979 without serious damage to the grass. After further checks on the establishment of the sward, it is proposed to lease the fields to adjoining farmers in the years to follow.

The tree planted areas were also soiled and forest transplants used at about 1.5m centres. The species included willow, alder, red oak, ash, larch, rowan and sycamore, all of which are indigenous to the area.

The overall cost of the project was £426,000 and based on a treated area of 50 ha gave a very economic cost of 0.85p per square metre.

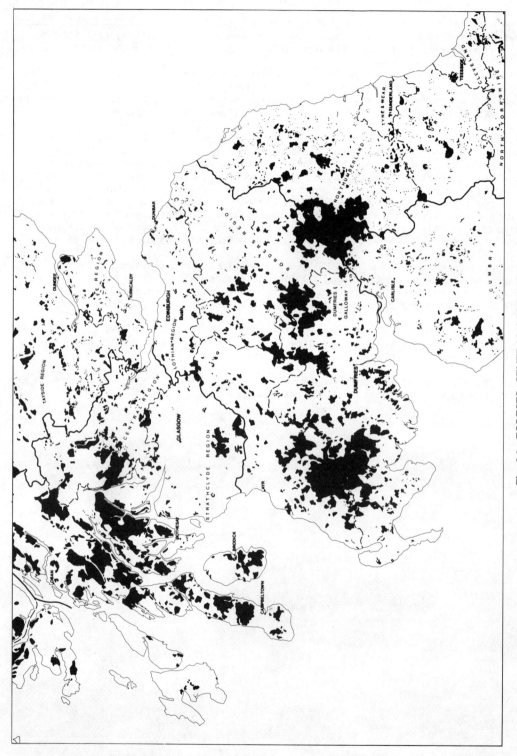

Fig. 6.1 FORESTS: CENTRAL SCOTLAND

CHAPTER 6
CITIES AND THEIR SYLVAN SETTING

W. G. Jeffrey
Forestry Commission
South Scotland Conservancy, Dumfries

Any opinions and conclusions expressed in this paper are those of the
writer and should not be taken to represent Forestry Commission policy.

ABSTRACT

This paper considers briefly the effect of man's development on the extent and
location of woodland in peri-urban areas in Scotland.

As a professional forester, rather than as an employee of the Forestry Commission,
the author looks at the place of forests, woods and trees in the peri-urban area,
and examines the Forester's scales of time, area and value in such areas against
those of other disciplines.

Finally the paper cites two examples of current tree planting/woodland establishment and considers ways in which the methods employed might be applied more widely
throughout Scotland.

KEYWORDS

Forestry Commission; Peri-urban areas; forest; wood; copse; return on investment; management systems.

HISTORY OF EXISTING WOODLANDS

Many writers (Tansley 1949, Stephens and Carlisle 1959) have examined the reduction
in the natural woodland cover of Scotland since the ice ages. In general too much
weight is attached to man's influence and too little to a worsening climate when
charting the change from perhaps as much as 60% in the Atlantic and sub-Boreal
periods to the treeless landscapes particularly south of the"Highland Line"revealed
by the early records and diarists of the 15th, 16th and 17th Centuries. Nevertheless the removal of the natural tree cover from Scotland's urban and peri-urban
areas can all be ascribed to man's needs for agricultural and development land.
This move from the 'Age of the occasional man' amid large forests to the 'Age of
the occasional tree' took from 3000 BC to 1500 AD. More recently there has been
what might be termed the "First Re-afforestation" and the "Second Re-afforestation".

The First Re-afforestation (1720-1850)

Complemented the intensification of lowland agriculture in the wake of the

51

Industrial Revolution and was fuelled by the city or colonial money of the improving landlords. It is these woodlands which have been such a valuable component of the lowland scene since Victorian times but whose conservation has been largely ignored until the last decade although it takes a century, not a decade, to bring balanced health and vigour to this element of the landscape.

The Second Re-afforestation (1919 continuing):

It took the First World War to finally convince the Nation of its need of a significant forest resource and to institute a Forestry Commission. The Second World War gave a further stronger impulsion to the extension of (re)afforestation into the hills and uplands, both by the Forestry Commission and the private sector of the Forestry industry. This second phase has included the re-awakening of active forest management, including the felling and replanting of some of the First Re-afforestation lowland woodlands, both by the private sector and the Forestry Commission. However, there have been virtually no additions to first generation woodlands, but numerous cases of losses for development or agricultural purposes particularly in the peri-urban areas.

There is a geological term "The aureole of contact metamorphism' which provides a useful parallel to the use of the term, 'peri-urban', in this paper. The urban area being equated with the igneous core and the peri-urban the encircling area of metamorphosed matrix rock. Forests, if present at all, help to set the outer limit of the aureole. The intrusion of the urban dweller into rural scene for recreation, for passage along communication corridors or by the lines and pipes of service industries is considered to be of merely local significance and therefore disregarded.

Function of the Forestry Commission

The Forestry Commission has two main functions statutarily based today in the Forestry Act 1967. Firstly, as Forest Authority it is responsible for the development and best use of the nation's forestry resources, the development of the wood-using industry, the encouragement of good forestry practice in the private sector, through advice and grant-aid, and also for plant health, research, training and legislation. Responsibility to Government is through three Forestry Ministers – the Minister of Agriculture and the Secretaries of State for Scotland and for Wales.

Secondly, as the Forest Enterprise, it manages on behalf of the nation a forest estate of 1,260,000 ha of which 63% is in Scotland, and in the management of which it is required, among other duties, to 'protect and enhance the environment; stimulate and support the local economy in areas of depopulation ...' and to provide recreational facilities (Forestry Commission 1980).

Current Forest Policy

The most recent Forest Policy Statement was made in the House of Commons by the Secretary of State for Scotland on the 10 December 1980, and the detailed procedures to implement that policy are still being worked out (Hansford 1980). But certainly in the short term the Forest Enterprise will have less money available for the purchase of new ground for peripheral interests such as provision of new recreational facilities, and inevitably there will be a concentration of managing the existing forests to provide timber for industry and to give employment in areas of depopulation. With less than 30% of its woodlands in production the Forestry Commission Enterprise continues to require an annual grant-in-aid, and to reduce the Forestry Commission's call on the Exchequer, the Government is also asking the Forestry Commission to realise some of its woodland assets. Among the woods to be considered for sale will be many of the smaller outlying blocks in the lowland

First Re-afforestation areas and which in some cases also lie within <u>peri-urban</u> <u>areas.</u>

For the future the Forestry Enterprise will therefore have a lessening role in the peri-urban areas, the Forestry Commission's Forestry Authority role will continue more or less as at present, and the private sector, i.e. the estate owners, farmers, local authorities and individual householders, will have the major role in the management of woods and trees within such areas.

FORESTS, WOODS AND TREES IN THE PERI-URBAN AREA

Foresters in Scotland are told by their English counterparts that they know little of population pressures and 'conservation lobbies', and if this is accepted then against a United Kingdom yardstick of urban, peri-urban and rural it could be contended that in Scotland there are only the peri-urban and rural categories.

Therefore, rather than look for special woodland categories within the peri-urban areas, it is better to consider the three main categories of tree cover, viz. forest, woodland and copses and spinneys (including single trees and hedgerows) and examine their contribution to the peri-urban environment.

Forest

A forest is an area used principally for the growing of trees which is large enough to have a significant effect on the locality in terms of appearance, employ-ment, wild life, climate, and depending upon the scale of the landscape a forest will have in Scotland a minimum size somewhere between 300 ha and 1000 ha. When in sustained production a coniferous forest will give employment to 1 man for every 100 ha and requre a technically trained forester in charge for every 2000 to 3000 ha.

Although there are in Scotland towns enfolded by forests, (Dalbeattie in SW Scotland is one very striking example) usually forests are located in the uplands some 30 or more Km from a city.

Wood

A wood is one component of a varied landscape. Whereas forests will generally have one or at most two primary functions, (if there are two one will invariably be the production of timber) woods are more subject to outside influences and are frequently multi-purpose. The production of wood for industry can be first or last on the priority list among the other uses; for amenity, shelter, recreation, sporting, conservation and even hygiene.

The title to this paper 'Cities and their Sylvan Setting' suggests that woodlands are an essential component of any well-endowed larger urban settlement. In Scot-land this is frequently the case but more by luck than inspired development, through cities' expansions having engulfed, and in places fortuitously retained, elements of the First Re-afforestation.

Copses, Spinneys and Trees

A wood is large enough (say a minimum size of 2 ha) to require ground inspection from several points before its boundaries can be determined; the third and final category of copses, spinneys and trees on the other hand can be given an overall appraisal from one or at most two points. Their primary function is seldom the production of timber, but ironically the greatest threat to many at this point in

time is the proliferation of wood-burning stoves in the houses of the more
affluent semi-urban and rural dwellers, and of chain saws in their garages.

FORESTERS' TIME, VALUE AND AREA APPRECIATION

One of the hazards associated with any form of specialist training is the gradual
separation from and eventually complete displacement and loss of recall of the
previous lay concepts. In forestry this is especially true of scales of time,
value and area.

Time

There are a few traditional forest areas where the local community are as aware of
the forest rhythms as the agricultural cycles but in Scotland these are restricted
to the centres of the First and Second Re-afforestations. Foresters therefore
invariably find in their ever-increasing contacts with the lay public and with other
disciplines that forest time scales require explanation. A politician thinks of a
week as a long time, to a planner five years is an infinity, but to the forester
it is commonplace to manage woodlands planted in Queen Victoria's reign and to
plant trees to be felled generations hence. The layman therefore looks upon the
woods and trees as a permanent feature of his environment while the forester knows
very well what stage they have reached in their life span.

The still standing woodlands of the First Re-afforestation are now entering their
geriatric phase but it is necessary to emphasise that in a demographic idiom it
is not a generation gap which exists but a dynastic period that has to be spanned,
and this is even more the case for broadleaves (or hardwoods) where the less
attractive adolescent phase can take upwards of sixty years.The better remaining
examples of the First Re-afforestation must therefore be husbanded carefully but
unswerving and persistent replanting and tending of the remainder is also a
necessity.

Values

Turning to the question of values, at any point in time a tree over, say 15 cm
diameter at breast height will have a value to a timber merchant. Today the 500
final crop trees on a hectare of coniferous wood at the end of its 40 to 70 year
rotation should be worth net about £4000, i.e. just under £10 apiece.

Hardwood trees have a very much wider range of values and at the extremes we can
take, firstly, a gnarled, heavily-branched specimen adjacent to buildings and with
embedded fencing wire and nails which will have a negative value equal to the cost
of felling it and removing it safely, which could amount to some hundreds of pounds;
and, secondly, a tree of the same venerable age but with a clean, straight and
wide bole of veneer quality with no felling and extraction problems which will have
a positive value of thousands of pounds.

The aesthete, however, may very much prefer the appearance of the gnarled specimen,
and the eccentric aesthete might even be prepared to spend hundreds of pounds in
copying the methods of the elite landscape gardeners of the 18th Century as
illustrated in Fig. to set a mature gnarled specimen into the garden of his
neo-Georgian villa.

What bearing do these rather extreme examples have on the management of woodlands
and trees in the peri-urban areas? Where trees have little or negative timber
value and present no danger to people or artefacts they can, if desired, be left
to fade gradually into oblivion. However, where trees and woods have a significant value, the wealth and charity of the owner will have a bearing on the time

which such trees can remain standing to satisfy his own and others' aesthetic and conservation values.

Area and Return on Forest Investment

Whether he be employed by the Forestry Commission or the private sector, for a forester a 3% return on the investment in real terms is the minimum target, although in the case of the Forestry Commission allowance is made where plantings on poorer ground are desirable in areas of depopulation. And I stress the 'real', which means the rate over and above the rate of inflation.

There are considerable economies of scale in forest management and in a background forestry paper prepared for the Central Scotland Woodland Project Steering Group it was demonstrated (Jeffrey 1977) that for the CSWP's typical poorer ground the rate of return for conifers fell from 3% to 0.3% as the block size decreased from 200 ha to 10 ha; that for better quality ground the return fell from 4.4% to 1.3%. and that it was on only the better quality ground that broadleaves could be considered as an economic crop but their return on the same block size would be from 1.2% to 0.4% poorer than conifers.

Despite the earlier definition of woodland, to many lay persons 10 ha is almost a forest and there are few areas of 40 ha of better quality ground (the 3% return break even point for conifers) in peri-urban areas where blocks of this size could be devoted to commercial forestry.

Assuming that the general size of the peri-urban woods is more likely to be 0.25 to 5 ha it can be seen not to be the province of the economic planter, private or state, but as by definition peri-urban woods are multi-purpose, as were those of the first re-afforestation there is every reason to suggest their management should be in the hands of the non-commercial forester, and that their ownership be related as directly as possible to those who enjoy the benefits of multi purpose use. The First Re-afforestation practitioners had two important advantages compared with the present day. Firstly, work was done within an estate under the control of one management and ownership, and secondly the discipline of a very much more localised population was under the owner's very firm direct or indirect control.

POINTS FOR FUTURE MANAGEMENT OF PERI-URBAN WOODLANDS

Against this background what factors has the non-commercial forester to consider in the First Re-afforestation consolidation and advance within peri-urban areas? There are the following six main factors:

1. The need to achieve a well distributed balance of age classes.

2. The realisation that forest areas and tree sites will ebb and flow with time, with some having to be put to other uses but equally land for planting being made available from other uses.

3. The management systems to be adopted will vary. Some sites where permanent tree cover is particularly important will require selective felling and replanting within the individual wood or some form of coppice treatment - to be likened to the treatment of a garden's herbaceous border as opposed to the complete bedding plant removal and replacement technique. But where number and variety allow, some woods can be clear felled and replanted progressively.

4. Grants are available from a number of sources for tree planting, including the Forestry Commission, Department of Agriculture for Scotland, Local Authorities and the Countryside Commission for Scotland, Nature Conservancy Council, and labour

may be available through youth and temporary employment schemes or various voluntary bodies. The most appropriate grant and scheme have to be selected, and
advantage also taken of any favourable fiscal regulations.

5. In the selection of species for planting or replanting, first define the
function or functions to be served - shelter, amenity, recreation, screen, conservation - then consider the desired life of the stand, and finally match the various
growth characteristics of the different species and varieties between themselves
and to the site. The main growth characteristics are final height, rate of growth,
tolerance to adverse site conditions, shape of tree, appearance of foliage, flowers
and fruits through the seasons of the year, and finally any bad effects of the
species on the environment, e.g. the root spread of poplars in relation to buildings.

6. Although the need to produce timber will seldom be high on the priority list,
as long as the other priorities are satisfied then the return from the final timber
sales should be as high as possible.

In this connection, of significance is the recent formation of a company in
North East Scotland which will produce ½ million young trees and bushes in 1981
and build up to 5 million by 1986, the trees to be of indigenous species with seed
or propagated material from selected sources. Matthews (1980) puts the matter in
a nutshell when he says "Finally it is a waste of the value of broadleaves to grow
trees with crooked stems and scrubby form. Tall straight trees with through axis
and erect habit are needed to repay the cost of planting and tending."

EXAMPLES OF TREE AND WOODLAND ESTABLISHMENT IN PERI-URBAN AREAS

Hobson's Colliery Site - County Durham

The very name itself conjures up a picture of dejection and gloom. This may very
well have been the case in the early fifties when the local parks superintendent,
Mr.George Tyrennan,persuaded the local Derwentside Councillors to employ a small
parks staff all the year round instead of seasonally in the spring and summer, and
to use the late autumn and winter period to plant up some of the worst eyesores.
More recently comprehensive redevelopment schemes have been taking place in the
area, but this earlier planting acted as a focal point for a section of this
redevelopment and is now a feature in its own right with its tree-clad slopes -
Corsican pine fringed with beech - providing a backcloth to a most attractive
public park and bowling green. In addition to making a silk purse out of a sow's
ear the District has a valuable timber resource which should provide a worthwhile
return in real terms on the original investment.

Central Scotland Woodland Project (CSWP) Lothian Regional Council(1978),Edwards
(1979)Sheldon (1980)

The project has just completed its second year of operation. The progress Reports
(CSWP 1980, CSWP 1981) contain many examples of the work in hand, but Community
Councils have not yet been actively involved. Lothian Region Council have now
drawn the SCWP's attention to a Community Council Scheme in Kirknewton, Midlothian
(Lothian Regional Council 1981) where planting in gardens and suitable open unused
spaces is now transforming this previously treeless village. "The experience at
Kirknewton showed that once residents understood that the right tree was to be
planted in the right place, and that trees were to be provided free and planted by
the Scouts, any opposition disappeared. So much support has been generated that
other sources of money are now being sought to continue the scheme beyond the
village".

The Lothian Region's Director of Physical Planning's first choice of name for this,

his brainchild, was Central Scotland Forest Landscape, however as the multi-disciplinary steering and working group deliberations progressed it became evident that woodland was more appropriate than forest, and that the Forestry Commission's role was primarily as Authority and not Enterprise.

These Groups looked critically at the grants for tree planting available from the various agencies, the labour which could be employed under the various Manpower Services Commission Schemes and concluded that the net cost of planting to owners could be very low indeed.

The recent Report of the Sub Committee on Forest Research of the House of Lords Select Committee on Science and Technology: (House of Lords 1980) states "(129). Secondly, experiments might be started in community forestry, the community managing is own woodland or plantations for its own needs, timber, firewood, amenity etc. The tradition and knowledge to do this have undoubtedly been lost almost everywhere but they could be revived with professional advice from the forestry industry or the Forestry Commission on contract. Ownership could be vested in local authorities, even parish councils, and might be obtained by bequest or in lieu of capital transfer tax. Some owners of neglected woodland might gladly lease them to the community for long terms. The scheme could revive interest in and appreciation of local woodlands, stimulate tree planting, preserve small woods and copses which had lost their original use but had acquired new amenity and recreation uses, and open up local markets for firewood, while at the same time maintaining the gentle diversity of Britain's woodland stock and their associated wildlife. Some cost would probably fall on the ratepayers but with judicious management the scheme might be made profitable, and in any event it would secure a future for local small woodlands and plantations now facing only decay".

The Central Scotland Woodland Project represents a flying start on their Lordships' thinking.

SUMMARY AND CONCLUSIONS

Tracing the origins of woodland in the peri-urban areas of Scotland shows it was established for different purposes and under a rural totalitarian regime.

The present role of the Forestry Commission in such areas is as Authority and it is suggested that the execution of forest policy here is the province of other interested national agencies, Local Authorities and private enterprise, rather than the Enterprise arm of the Forestry Commission.

Definition of 'forests', 'woods' and 'copses', together with an appreciation of the view time, value and area are necessary in evaluating the role of trees in the peri-urban environment.

Finally, sylvan perfection cannot be achieved overnight. In the examples cited, caring and perseverance are the most important factors and there must be a continuing and sustained effort by each generation to provide Cities in their Sylvan Settings for their children, their grandchildren and the succeeding generations.

REFERENCES

Forestry Commission 1980. The Forestry Commission Objectives Policy and
    Procedures Paper No. 1 FC Edinburgh
Hansard 1980 Forest Policy Statement by the Secretary of State for Scotland
    Hansard Vol. 995 No. 15 Cols 1405-1406 10 December 1980

House of Lords, 1980 Rep of Select Comm on Science and Technology - Scientific
    Aspects of Forestry Vol 1 - Report para 129 HMSO
Jeffrey, W.G. 1977 Background Forestry Paper to Central Scotland Forest Landscape
    Committee Unpubl. Forestry Commission, Dumfries
Matthews, J.D. 1980 The Place of Broadleaved Trees in the Uplands of Britain.
    Quarterly Journal of Forestry Vol. LXXV(2) pp.105-106
Steven, H.M. and Carlisle, A. 1959 The Native Pinewoods of Scotland Ch.2 Oliver
    and Boyd, Edinburgh
Tansley, Sir A.G. 1949 The British Islands and their Vegetation Vol. 1 Chs. 7
    and 8 2nd ed. CUP. London

                CSWP REFERENCES

CSWP 1980 First Interim Report Feb. 1979-Jan 1980 CSWP Falkirk
CSWP 1981 Second Interim Report Feb 1980-Jan 1981 CSWP Falkirk
Edwards, B. 1979 Central Scotland Woodlands Project The Greening of a Moorland
    Plateau Landscape Design No. 128 Nov. 1979 pp.20-22
Lothian Regional Council 1978. Central Scotland Woodlands Project Report of the
    Steering Group Lothian Regional Council, Edinburgh
Lothian Regional Council 1981. CSWP - Action by Community Councils Unpubl. paper.
    Lothian Regional Council, Edinburgh
Sheldon, J.C. The Central Scotland Woodlands Project A Plan for Land Use and
    Landscape Renewal Arboricultural Journal Vol. 4. No. 1 pp.41-50 Apr. 1980.

Fig. 6.2 SIR HENRY STEUART'S PLANTING MACHINE

COMMENT ON MORNING SESSION BY SYMPOSIUM DISCUSSANT

Joy Tivy
University of Glasgow

The preceding papers have highlighted the particular involvement of four different
types and levels of government in the problems of 'conserving and improving the
environmental quality (particularly in respect of appearance and recreational
value) of the 'Countryside round Urban Areas in Scotland'. Protection of the
Countryside, now a statutorily defined and delimited area, is the dominant note
struck. Indeed at times the negative impact of the town on the country has been
stressed to an extent that might suggest the former to be intrinsically ugly
(undesirable), the latter beautiful (desirable)!

Several varying though not mutually exclusive attitudes to the role and value of
what is called the 'peri-urban' area have emerged. The Countryside Commission for
Scotland has defined it as the zone 5-10 miles wide immediately adjacent to the
urban area and regards it as a particular type of Countryside insofar as it is
located and functions within urban structures. Its recreational role, in balance
with other functions, should be to serve the needs of the contiguous urban people
by providing a local neighbourhood park function for which it has been suggested
there is probably considerable unexploited potential. And the Commission is
already heavily committed to the area because of the location of Country Parks.

It would have been interesting to know how far local authorities share Mr. McDonald's
perception of the area as the 'town's back garden' whose countryside appearance
has been marred by urban-type intrusions and a decline in the agricultural base
and his concern for the image that the peri-urban area conveys to the prospective
tourist or industrialist.

Up-to-date the Scottish Development Agency has made a greater aesthetic impact on
the peri-urban area than probably any other agency. Its involvement is, however,
the result of the peri-urban concentration of derelict land and of potential 'greenfield sites' for industrial location or relocation (for both of which it has direct
responsibilities) rather than of an intrinsic concern for the area per se. In
contrast, it is a zone from which it appears the Forestry Commission may be, because
of recent legislation designed to rationalise timber production in the U.K., with-
drawing. The problem of the conservation of the economic and aesthetic value of
the scattered copses, shelter belts, and small woods, so characteristic of the
peri-urban fringe, however, will remain.

The peri-urban zone is an area for which there is no one comprehensive planning

agency; a situation which may create more problems than have been identified or
solved unless there is active co-operation among the agencies involved. It is
exacerbated by the varying and often nebulous concepts of the peri-urban area which
have been expressed. The area is situated at the interface between two contrasting
and dynamic areas. Essential to its character and to what have been defined as
its problems is that it is a zone of transition, and tension, between town and
country. As such it exhibits the 'edge effects' of the classic ecological zone of
transition (ecotone) in that it not only contains urban and non-urban elements but
those characteristic - indeed diagnostic - of the zone itself.

In trying to analyse the extent, characteristics and problems of the peri-urban
area it might be useful to make a distinction between the urban fringe where
urban impact is direct and where the function in the past as in the present, was
primarily to serve the adjacent city or town: and the urban shadow, the maximum
extent of the residential and recreational commuting zone. In the latter the
aesthetic problems arising from urban impact on the Countryside are different but
none the less important. Questions of access to land, provisions of outdoor recreation facilities, and management to minimise the deterioration of the environmental quality of forest, agriculture, and moorland must, particularly in Central
Scotland, increasingly exercise the Countryside Commission for Scotland, Forestry
Commission and local authorities alike. In this respect a 'landscape element'
very characteristic of the peri-urban fringe in Central Scotland, which has been
overlooked, is that of the small water-body whose potential for urban-based
recreation (not least bank-fishing and wildlife conservation) may be considerably
greater than that of the land area. Indeed in both instances, however, constraints
may well be greater than the assumed potential for recreational use.

While the town-countryside gradient has been stressed, it is perhaps well to remind
ourselves that the peri-urban area in Central Scotland is not only extensive, but
is highly fragmented, and except on the most southern and northern limits is made
up of islands of varying scale between numerous towns of disparate size. In some
locations it is a broad transition zone, in others it is barely discernible and
there is a marked discontinuity between town and country. Further, it varies
considerably in character and in the mix of landscape elements dependent upon,
the form and agricultural capability of the land, the urban land use history, the
socio-economic characteristics of the contiguous residential areas, urban and
countryside land tenure, and the past and current planning policies of the Regions
and Districts involved.

Finally one is left perhaps with the impression that all those concerned with the
appearance of the peri-urban area and the preservation of Countryside within it,
may be in a Catch-22 situation; first, because of an implicit assumption that the
countryside (rural) and urban functions can be clearly separated; second, because
establishment of a fixed Countryside Boundary, in an indeterminate and dynamic
transition zone, might in time result in more of the Countryside Commission for
Scotland's funds being allocated to urban rather than peri-urban and countryside
areas.

CHAPTER 7
AGRICULTURE ON THE URBAN EDGE

Department of Agriculture and
Fisheries for Scotland

ABSTRACT

Since 1945 Government has taken a keen interest in the preservation of agricultural
land. Loss of such land to development has been inevitable and has taken place
mainly in Central Scotland, an area of coincidence of prime agricultural land and
major unborn settlement. This paper outlines current Government policy and
activity in giving advice to planning authorities through the Department of agriculture and Fisheries for Scotland.

KEYWORDS

Loss of prime quality agricultural land; development planning; government policy;
good and bad planning; the urban edge.

The Government has, since the last war, taken a keen interest in the preservation
of agricultural land, especially high-grade land, and in the maintenance of agricultural production. The nature of that interest has varied over the years but the
major emphasis at the moment is that of guardianship of a scarce resource. Loss
of agricultural land has, of course, to be accepted in some instances in the face
of other national and local demands, but a national conservation policy remains
essential in the face of the all too prevalent temptation to regard land, especially in Scotland, as an expendable resource.

The rate of land loss over the period 1971-1979 is illustrated in Table 7.1.

The trend in terms of area of land lost appears to be downwards, but the percentage
of prime land (that is of agricultural grades A+, A and B+) remains high.$_2$

The relevance of this problem to the urban fringe becomes obvious when one looks
more closely at agricultural land quality in relation to the major built-up areas
of Scotland (Fig. 7.1.).

The cities more or less site in the middle of the major reservoirs of top-grade
agricultural land and every expansion, whether for housing, industry or recreation,
puts pressure on the surviving agricultural resource. It has to be borne in mind
that prime quality land represents only 7 per cent of the land surface of Scotland
and in terms of cultivable land still only 8 per cent.

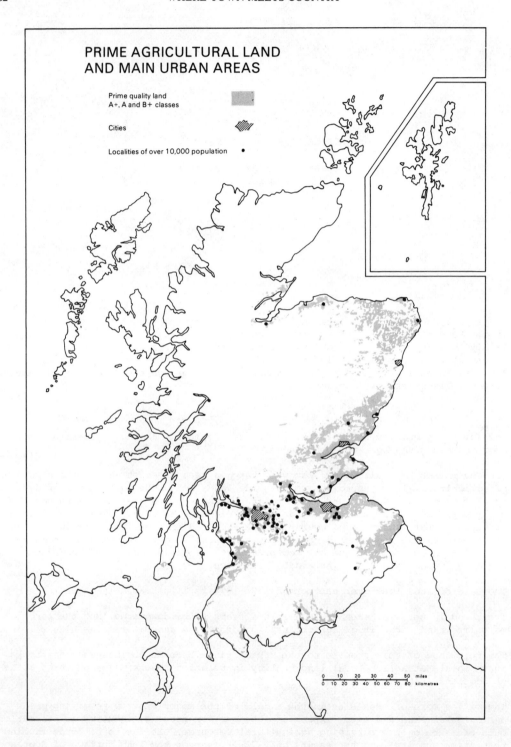

Fig. 7.1   PRIME AGRICULTURAL LAND AND THE URBAN AREAS OF SCOTLAND

TABLE 7.1   Agricultural Land - Annual Losses to Development: Scotland
1971 to 1979.   Hectares.

	Prime quality land (Grade A+, A and B+)	Other agricultural land	Total
1971	818	503	1,321
1972) 1973)	1,184	1,099	2,283
1974	687	356	1,043
1975	523	425	948
1976	477	904	1,381
1977	548	514	1,062
1978	548	506	1,054
1979	472	434	906
Total	5,257	4,741	9,998

Source: Estimates by Department of Agriculture and Fisheries for Scotland

Note: Estimated existing (1981) total of Prime Quality Land in Scotland is
520,000 ha.

The location and extent of agricultural land lost to urban development is illustrated in detail in Fig. 7.2, which is taken from a recent Government study of
Strathclyde Region.[2]   Erosion of agricultural land is seen to be occurring around
the entire edge of the Clydeside conurbation.   The major losses are to housing and
industry.

Actual loss of land is by no means the whole of the agricultural problem, and the
proper management of land on the city fringe is of the utmost importance for
agriculture.   This paper, however, concentrates on the effects on agriculture of
good and bad planning.

Bad planning may take the form of:

a)   approving developments on the urban fringe which by their nature or through
their design cause lower production in adjoining agricultural units or create
uncertainty about the future of agriculture.   Examples might be certain forms of
industrial production ("bad neighbours") or unsuitable layout of housing estates
facilitating vandalism, stock worrying etc.

b)   excessive allocation ("zoning") of land for development, in development plans

c)   unsuitable allocation or designation of land for development, i.e. without
taking sufficient account of the quality of land or the effect on individual farm
units.

Government policy simply put is that:

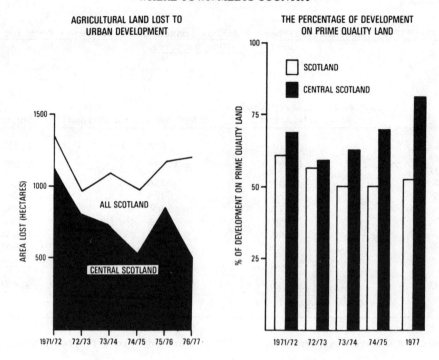

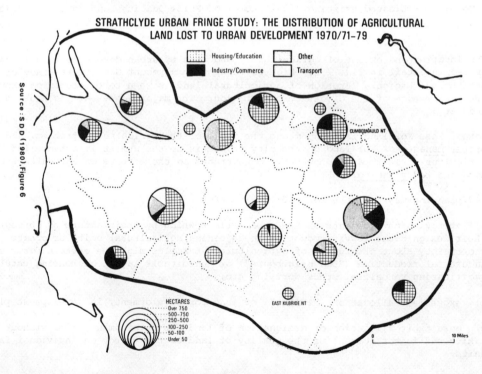

Fig. 7.2   LOSS OF AGRICULTURAL LAND TO DEVELOPMENT: CLYDESIDE CONURBATION

a) no more agricultural land should be taken for development than is necessary.

b) Where it is necessary, poorer land should always be taken in preference to better land.

Of course, the policy requires to be much more specifically stated - and this will be done in new national"planning guidelines" expected to be published in 1981. The issuing of "planning guidelines" is a continuing process, the first set of guidelines having been issued in 1977.4 Government guidance, which aims at putting the issues against the national perspective, includes:

a) information about the problem (in the form of "Land Use Summary Sheets" of various kinds including sheets on agriculture and housing).

b) advice on development planning, i.e. structure and local plans, including safeguards for agricultural land. These take the form of requirements for the planning authority to consult D.A.F.S. staff before finalising development plans.

c) advice on development control, including safeguards for agricultural land. These take the form of procedures for the call-in of development proposals for the Secretary of State's decision, where agricultural land would be seriously affected.

Government advice in this field can only be rather broad-brush, and Government intervention is bound to be preventive and negative rather than creative. The really positive initiatives lie with local planning authorities and developers, e.g. along the following lines.

a) actively re-examining existing wasteland and inner city sites, to see what potential they offer for necessary development to reduce the need for "greenfield" sites.

b) "planning the urban edge" in order to -

- take account of and steer necessary development to the right places

- provide security for farmers to continue farming productively

- identify and reinforce existing natural and man made boundaries, such as steep slopes, urban motorways, canals, etc. (so as to check sporadic development)

- to recognise the public's need for access and recreation.

The place of green belts onthe city fringe and the place of agriculture within them is a large subject, strictly speaking outside the Department's remit. Nevertheless what was said in Circular No. 40/19605 (which remains the current official advice on planning the green belt) is still worth reading. Productive agriculture on the city fringe is an objective worth pursuing not just for its own sake (although that is of considerable importance) but also because of its contribution to amenity and a satisfactory environment.

REFERENCES

Scottish Development Department Circular 19/1977 (1977) Land Use Summary Sheet No. 1 on Agriculture summarises the factors which determine the classification of land.

Thomas, M.F. & Coppock, J.T. (1980). <u>Land Assessment in Scotland,</u> Aberdeen
     University Press, Aberdeen, gives details of the classification together with
     a critique.
<u>Agricultural Land and Urban Development</u> (unpublished monograph) Central Planning
     Group, Scottish Development Department, 1980.
"Development" is defined in section 19 of the Town and Country Planning Scotland
     Act 1972. As employed in this paper it is urban development, in the
     following categories - roads; housing; schools; prisons; hospitals;
     crematoria etc.; industrial and commercial; other and unclassified.
Scottish Development Department Circular 19/1977.
Department of Health for Scotland Circular Bo.40/1960.

CHAPTER 8
PROBLEMS OF AGRICULTURE IN PERI-URBAN AREAS.

S. Alexander Ross
West of Scotland Agricultural College (Clyde Area)

ABSTRACT

This paper examines the problems experienced by and the opportunities afforded to
farmers by virtue of the location of their enterprises on the urban fringe in
Scotland. Some background statistics are provided.

KEYWORDS

urban fringe - expanding, established or static; problems and opportunities of
farming; background statistics.

1. PROBLEMS AND OPPORTUNITIES.

The problems and the opportunities of farming close to large populations differ
widely from area to area depending on a number of factors. Some of these are:-
whether the urban fringe is expanding actively or is established and static;
whether it is industrial or residential; whether low density suburban private
housing or high density city overspill estates; and reaction of the farmer to
nuisance and opportunity.

Expanding Urban Fringe

Where the urban fringe is expanding actively as in the development of new towns
it is necessary for a number of farms to be vacated at an early stage of the
development. Since all the released land is unlikely to be required at this stage
the developing authority is generally able to lease some of the land on short term
tenancy to the remaining farmers. This allows short term expansion possibilities
which is generally in the form of increased cropping.

Uncertainty regarding when and if such land will be ultimately required for development makes medium to long term planning impossible. This results in the application of little if any lime and basic fertilisers and the adoption of poor farming
practice.

The problem generally occurs when these short term leases expire, because during
the period of expansion in cropping, there is a tendency for a less intensive
system of stock farming to develop and thus financial turn-over to fall.

Where the urban fringe is expanding actively, aggravation is often caused by civil engineering contractors carrying out work at inappropriate times or in inappropriate ways. This is generally due to contractors being ignorant of farming requirements and problems.

Where the urban fringe is expanding, farms can seldom be managed in a way which will express their full potential.

Where the Urban Fringe is Static

In most situations the urban fringe is relatively static and problems are of a different nature.

The main problem is the public. One person walking through a field to exercise a dog may not do any harm, but allowing one can result in many doing likewise and damage resulting. Conflict can result from trying to explain to a person why he or she should not use a field to exercise themselves or their dogs.

In many situations it is possible to allow public to walk over land provided they observe the countryside code of practice. The main problems which result from the public walking through fields are:- distressing grazing cattle or sheep; leaving gates insecurely fixed which result in stock straying or mixing; damaging fencing through climbing it rather than using gates; interfering with water troughs thus damaging the ballcock and causing overflow and flooding; dogs chasing rabbits, hares etc. and damaging dykes; dropping plastic bags which can result in deaths when eaten by stock. There have been extreme cases where animals have been wounded by air guns and even knives.

The Countryside Commission and other bodies are doing all they can to educate the public to use the countryside sensibly.

Most of the problems are created by carelessness but some are deliberate destructiveness. The grazing of livestock and making of hay sometimes becomes impossible. There are cases where young people damage hay bales at one end of the field while the farmer is still working at the other end.

Dumping rubbish can cause damage to machinery and can injure or damage the health of livestock. Balers, combines and forage harvesters are the items of equipment most frequently damaged by material being thrown into fields of dumped in fields.

Security is a problem on farms in urban areas. It is not possible to keep all doors locked or for someone always to be at the farm. It is not uncommon for youths to call at the farm house for a drink of water or similar excuse. If they get no reply it is an opportunity to prowl around.

Fire risk is of course greater in urban areas. Hay and straw storage requires to be restricted to small quantities not adjacent to buildings housing animals. Adequate insurance cover is of course an essential.

Transporting material or moving stock from fields to the farm steading or vice versa can be a problem on busy roads. Heavy traffic particularly at rush hours and on summer week-ends can seriously interfere with harvest work.

Winter work on wet fields can result in mud being carried onto the roads. Clearing it is the responsibility of the farmer and this is a bigger problem in urban than in country areas.

Farming near to the urban fringe also has business management problems. Higher wages and better working conditions are generally available in towns or on industrial sites than can be offered on farms. There is therefore a tendency for workers to be attracted away from farming.

Land near to the urban fringe tends to have a higher value. This is due to a number of factors such as, a 'hope' value for long term development; social advantages of being near to a town; hobby farming by business men; land for ponies, riding schools, etc.

Advantages and Opportunities

Farming close to the urban fringe may have opportunities and advantages not avail-able in true rural situations.

A big market close to the production unit provides an opportunity to retail milk, eggs, chickens, potatoes, vegetables, etc. This may be by taking the goods to the public or by the public coming to the farm. Some farmers may complain about the disturbance by public calling at inconvenient times to purchase produce. However they may complain more if there were no callers for such cash sales. In many situations there is scope for this opportunity to be exploited further by better organising the production, buying and marketing of appropriate products.

There may be a market for hay and oats for ponies and alternative land uses for horse grazing, horse liveries and other recreational purposes.

Casual labour for seasonal work and tradesmen may be more easily available.Exper-tise and quality however are often insufficient to competently operate some mechanical equipment now used on farms.

An early warning of an animal in distress or in need of attention is often given by passers-by or people able to see the animals from their homes.

It has the advantage of being nearer to schools, recreational facilities and job opportunities for members of the family.

Education

Most farmers realise that the public wish to make greater use of the countryside and the majority wish to co-operate in making this possible. Farmer reaction to the presence of the public is variable. What is considered a nuisance by one may present an opportunity to another.

Housing and industrial development tends to take place on the better quality land best suited for arable cropping and intensive grass growing. These intensive systems of farming can be very seriously affected by certain actions by the public and sometimes even by their presence.

Farmers on the urban fringe already have problems with traffic and the public, thus every effort is being made to encourage the public to use true rural situations for walking and recreation, preferably hill land.

The Countryside Commission arrange "Family Days on the Farm" and like most other bodies, take the public to farms some distance from the urban fringe.

An education policy is required with positive management techniques to allow the public access to the countryside with minimum infringement on farming and particu-larly those in urban situations.

2.   BACKGROUND STATISTICS ON AGRICULTURE AND HORTICULTURE IN DISTRICTS
CLOSE TO LARGE POPULATIONS

In looking at any aspect of Scottish Agriculture, the physical constraints of
climate, land quality and topography must be recognised as having a very strong
influence. The high rainfall, predominance of rough grazing and short growing
season, dictate a pastural type of farming over much of the country giving a high
degree of self sufficiency in livestock and livestock products.

Another factor influencing the pattern of food production is the way in which
population is concentrated into a few large conurbations. In those districts where
agriculture and horticulture compete for land with urban uses and "co-exist", there
are benefits (plus factors) and problems (minus factors), for primary producers.
The benfits accrue through proximity to markets and also to a pool of casual, or
part-time labour. The latter advantage is particularly relevant during the present
recession when labour is more likely to be available than attracted to better paid
urban employment. The proximity to markets can also be interpreted in the broadest
sense, to include the demand for amenity and recreation, ranging from equestrian
activities, to the provision of a local milk bar.

The disadvantages also take a variety of different forms ranging from the mere
nuisance of city dwellers, ignorant of the needs of farmers, to wholesale damage
to crops, livestock and property, including the not uncommon hazard of loss through
fires.

The extent to which farmers benefit from opportunities, or suffer nuisance, is
something that defies easy analysis. Both urban and rural areas contain a variety
of different characteristics that cannot be measured in terms of distance from the
city centre. Human reactions are also infinitely variable and what is a nuisance
to one individual may present an opportunity to another.

The picture shown in the tables that follow is intended to provide a background to
an appraisal of agriculture and its relationships with town and city. It emphasises
the ground that is common to all farmers in a region where climate and terrain place
limits on farming opportunities. But it also shows that initiative and enterprise
can lead to a wide variety of farm and horticultural production exploiting both
natural advantages and local markets.

The districts chosen for illustration (see Table 8:1) are somewhat arbitrary but
they do give a good coverage in both the east and west of Scotland. Two features
are common to these districts. All are producers of fruit and vegetables and all
are not too distant from markets in Glasgow, Dundee and Edinburgh.

TABLE 8.1   Population in Selected Local Government Regions and
Districts in Scotland - 1971 Census

Region or District		Number of Persons '000	Per cent of Scotland Population
North Clyde	Dumbarton	78.7	
	City of Glasgow	982.3	
	Clydebank	58.8	
	Bearsden & Milngavie	35.9	
	Strathkelvin	77.5	
	Cumbernauld & Kilsyth	45.6	
	Monklands	109.6	
	Motherwell	161.6	
	TOTAL	1550.0	29.6
South Clyde	Hamilton	104.4	
	East Kilbride	74.2	
	Eastwood	49.8	
	Renfrew	202.9	
	Inverclyde	109.4	
	TOTAL	540.7	10.3
Lanark	TOTAL	53.5	1.0
Angus & Dundee City	Angus	84.2	
	Dundee City	197.4	
	TOTAL	281.6	5.4
Fife	Dunfermline	120.5	
	Kirkcaldy	145.0	
	North East Fife	61.6	
	TOTAL	327.1	6.3
Lothians	East Lothian	77.4	
	Edinburgh	476.6	
	Mid Lothian	79.7	
	West Lothian	111.8	
	TOTAL	745.6	14.3
TOTAL OF SELECTED REGIONS/DISTRICTS		3498.5	66.9
TOTAL SCOTLAND		5229.0	100.0

Source: Scottish Abstract of Statistics No. 9 - 1980.   The Scottish Office.

TABLE 8.2   Crops, Grass and Rough Grazing in Selected Districts
in Scotland, 1978

District	Crops and Grass	Rough Grazing	Total Agricultural Area	Percentage of Rough Grazing
	'000 hectares			
North Clyde	30.5	44.3	74.8	59
South Clyde	41.7	26.4	68.1	39
Lanark	43.6	71.5	115.1	62
Angus and City of Dundee	95.7	91.1	186.8	49
Fife	86.1	8.5	94.6	9
Lothians	87.5	40.3	127.8	32

Source: Agricultural Statistics Scotland 1978, DAFS.

The three districts in the east of Scotland cover a greater area than those in the
west. However, with the exception of Fife, all have a high proportion of rough
grazing, which is characteristic of farming in most Scottish counties. The national
average for Scotland is over 72 per cent in rough grazings, so that farming in the
districts shown is more favourably placed in this respect, than much of the rest
of Scotland.

TABLE 8.3   Grazing, Cereals and Potatoes in Selected Districts
of Scotland, 1978

District	Grass	Total Cereals	Seed Potatoes	Ware Potatoes
North Clyde	25.1	4.5	–	0.2
South Clyde	35.9	4.8	neg	0.2
Lanark	34.7	6.9	0.1	0.1
Angus and City of Dundee	36.6	43.5	5.9	1.9
Fife	35.4	40.4	2.2	2.4
Lothians	37.2	42.6	0.6	1.9

Source: Agricultural Statistics Scotland 1978, DAFS.

The areas devoted to major crops and grass, again emphasise the different patterns
of farming between the east and west. Grassland predominates in the west with
relatively minor areas devoted to cereals and potatoes. Conversely, the east has
substantial areas devoted to cereals and potatoes, with seed potato production an
important activity. Even so, there is still a large area of grassland in the
eastern counties with grazing livestock of some importance. The relationship of
crops to livestock is seen in Table 8.4.

TABLE 8.4   Numbers of Cattle, Sheep, Pigs and Poultry in Selected
Districts of Scotland, 1978

District	Dairy Cows	Beef Cows	Ewes	Sows	Total Poultry
	'000				
North Clyde	9.8	8.0	49.9	0.8	180.0
South Clyde	23.5	9.2	36.4	0.4	142.2
Lanark	16.9	11.5	106.0	0.4	170.4
Angus and City of Dundee	6.6	16.9	65.0	2.2	637.2
Fife	10.9	12.2	35.6	2.2	3501.6
Lothians	7.9	11.3	87.0	7.4	1872.9

Source: Agricultural Statistics Scotland 1978, DAFS.

Allowing for the differences in agricultural area in the various districts, the
emphasis on grazing livestock is greater in the west, particularly in the case of
dairy cows and ewes. Nonetheless, the importance of pastoral farming in the east
is still very evident.

With pigs and poultry there is an obvious link with the ability to grow cereals in
the east. Although both forms of intensive livestock production can and do, rely
on bought-in concentrate feeds, the growing and home mixing of cereals plays an
important part in feeding pigs and poultry.

TABLE 8.5   The Importance of Fruit and Vegetables in Selected
Districts of Scotland (The "Garden" of Scotland)

District	Straw-berries	Rasp-berries	Soft Fruit	Rhubarb	Outdoor Lettuce	Tomatoes under glass	Total Vegetables
	hectares						
North Clyde	2.9	2.1	17.9	11.2	9.3	2.6	34.6
South Clyde	12.5	5.8	25.0	83.1	26.2	7.9	158.4
Lanark	25.3	21.3	91.4	0.1	18.8	18.5	34.4
Angus and City of Dundee	391.1	1239.3	1657.8	38.2	2.5	0.8	1625.8
Fife	81.2	74.6	167.7	0.4	7.6	0.7	1673.1
Lothians	46.3	12.7	82.5	4.3	26.6	2.1	1574.8

Source: Agricultural Statistics Scotland 1978, DAFS.

In looking at areas devoted to horticultural crops the level of investment and
output per hectare must be considered, as the level of intensity and cash output
depends on the type of crop grown. For example 18 hectares of tomatoes relative
to 18 hectares of lettuce in Lanark represents a vastly greater financial output.

Although the west is better known for producing the cream that goes with the
strawberries produced in the east, it does have its own specialities. Tomatoes

under glass, hold pride of place and are a good example of the way in which local growers have built up a reputation for quality and freshness. This "quality" image enables Clyde valley growers to command a substantial premium with a large proportion of the crop sold direct to retail outlets without recourse to the wholesale market.

Another interesting crop is rhubarb which is grown very close to the Glasgow city centre.

Some vegetables and soft fruit are grown in the west, but the east dominates production of both, with most of the soft fruit produced in the Dundee area, where canning and preserving industries have been a long standing tradition.

It would probably be true to say that the "garden" is greener in the east!

Size of Holdings and Labour Use

Although statistical information on agriculture in the United Kingdom is very comprehensive, one aspect that the computer age has not managed to document fully, is the extent to which occupiers farm more than one holding. In 1978 there were about 31,000 holdings in Scotland of which 11,000 were classified as part or sparetime i.e. around 20,000 full-time. Full-time occupiers were 15,000 in number, which by simple division provides one and one third holdings per full-time occupier. At a part and spare-time level, 8,000 occupiers farm 11,000 holdings or 1.28 holdings per occupier.

The number of holdings run by farm managers is estimated at around 800 for Scotland. Thus the general conclusion is that a considerable number of occupiers of land, farm more than one holding.

In the tables that follow the approach to farm size is based on the area of land farmed by occupiers rather than size of holding, although the number of holdings is quoted to give the complete picture.

TABLE 8.6   Number of Holdings and Number of Occupiers in Selected
Districts of Scotland, 1978

District	Number of Occupiers				Per Cent Full Time	Total Holdings	Holdings per Occupier
	Full Time	Part Time	Spare Time	Total Occupiers			
North Clyde	377	74	81	532	71	701	1.32
South Clyde	524	78	85	687	76	876	1.28
Lanark	480	70	104	654	73	848	1.30
Angus and City of Dundee	648	113	119	880	74	1179	1.34
Fife	554	96	111	761	73	984	1.29
Lothians	579	116	127	822	70	1146	1.39

Source: Agricultural Statistics Scotland 1978, DAFS.

In the districts covered in Table 8.5 there is a similar pattern. The proportion of full-time occupiers to total occupiers falls in a very narrow range between 70 and 76 per cent. This group of occupiers is obviously responsible for a very high

percentage of total output. Numbers of part and spare time occupiers are similar
in most districts and there is a very narrow range of variation in the number
of holdings per occupier, between 1.29 and 1.39.

TABLE 8.7   Area of Crops + Grass and Total Agricultural Area per
Occupier in Selected Districts of Scotland, 1978

	Area per occupier		
District	Crops and Grass	Rough Grazing	Total Agricultural Area
	hectares		
North Clyde	57.3	83.2	140.5
South Clyde	60.7	38.5	99.2
Lanark	66.6	109.4	176.0
Angus and City of Dundee	108.7	103.5	212.2
Fife	113.1	11.1	124.2
Lothian	106.5	49.0	155.5

Source: Agricultural Statistics Scotland 1978, DAFS.

Although rough grazing has an important bearing on the potential of farms in the
districts analysed, by European and even UK standards, the average area of crops
and grass represents a reasonable size of business.

However, it is evident that the farms in the three eastern districts are much
bigger than those in the west. They also have the advantage of being able to grow
a wider range of arable crops.

TABLE 8.8   Number of Hired Workers, Including Family, on Farms in
Selected Districts of Scotland, 1978

District	Number of Workers				Of Which family workers	Family as per cent of total
	Full Time	Part Time	Casual	Total		
North Clyde	492	150	163	804	285	35
South Clyde	734	224	340	1298	409	32
Lanark	817	174	190	1181	358	30
Angus and City of Dundee	2018	279	602	2899	349	12
Fife	2285	458	272	3015	412	14
Lothians	2128	471	287	2886	419	15

Source: Agricultural Statistics Scotland 1978, DAFS

The more favourable farm structure of holdings in the eastern districts is reflected
in the pattern of labour used. The size of business in the east enables considerably

more full-time workers to be employed. Part-time labour is important to all farms, but particularly so in Fife and the Lothians. Casual labour is obviously linked with fruit and vegetables and holdings in Angus and South Clyde rely heavily on this type of help. Providing employment for members of the Family is a tradition in farming and horticulture, although on the larger holdings in the east, this represents a relatively small share of the total labour input.

A further perspective on total employment is given in Tables 8.8 and 8.9 where all labour including that of the Farmer and his wife is considered.

TABLE 8.9   Total Labour Input Including Occupier, Spouse and Hired
                Labour for Selected Areas in Scotland, 1978

District	Occupier and Spouse		Hired Labour		
	All Occupiers	Spouses(1) of Occupier	Full Time	Part-Time and Casual	(Of which family workers)
North Clyde	532	251	492	313	(285)
South Clyde	687	337	734	564	(409)
Lanark	654	285	817	364	(358)
Angus and City of Dundee	880	223	2018	881	(349)
Fife	761	211	2285	730	(412)
Lothians	822	238	2128	758	(419)

Source: Agricultural Statistics Scotland 1978, DAFS.

TABLE 8.10   Total Labour Input Expressed as a Proportion of All
                Occupiers for Selected Areas in Scotland, 1978.

District	Occupier and Spouse		Hired Labour		
	All Occupiers	Spouses(1) of Occupier	Full Time	Part-Time and Casual	(Of Which family workers)
North Clyde	1.00	0.47	0.92	0.59	(0.54)
South Clyde	1.00	0.49	1.07	0.82	(0.60)
Lanark	1.00	0.44	1.25	0.56	(0.55)
Angus and City of Dundee	1.00	0.25	2.29	1.00	(0.40)
Fife	1.00	0.28	2.00	0.96	(0.54)
Lothians	1.00	0.29	2.59	0.92	(0.51)

Source: Agricultural Statistics Scotland 1978, DAFS.

(1) The figure for farm work carried out by spouse of occupier, does not indicate the proportion of the time spent on farm work.

Table 8.8 shows the absolute figures for labour employed on holdings in the selected districts. These indicate the relatively greater importance of the family (i.e occupier, spouse and family workers) on the smaller sized business in western districts.

In Table 8.10 the same figures are expressed as a proportion of All Occupiers (i.e
full-time, part-time and spare-time). Thus, for every occupier, between one
quarter and one half of the wives worked on the holding, with working wives more
common in the western districts. In all areas, except North Clyde, there was at
least one full-time hired worker for every occupier, with at least 2 and up to 3
workers in the eastern districts.

PERI-URBAN FARMING BIBLIOGRAPHY

Brandsen, S. "The Battle of Chertsey" Farmers Weekly, March 13 1981.

Butcher, F. "After the road builders, tenant fights four year battle for
    compensation" Farmers Weekly, October 10 1981.

Coleman, A. and Feaver, I. "Farm Vandals - who carries the can?" Farmers Weekly.
    July 4 1980.

Crofts, T. "Creeping Blight is a hidden danger" British Farmer and Stockbreeder,
    April 26 1980.

Dodd, P. "A tattered fringe - the demise of farming in the green belt" British
    Farmer and Stockbreeder, December 6 1980.

Skinner, D.N. "A situation report on Green Belts in Scotland". Countryside
    Commission for Scotland. Occasional Paper No. 8. 1976.

Taylor, D. "Its no longer worth the trouble to farm" British Farmer and Stockbreeder,
    February 2 1980.

University of Reading, Department of Agricultural Economics and Management. "Milton
    Keynes 1975 - Farming in and out of the Designated Area". Miscellaneous
    Study No. 61. 1975.

Johnson, G. "Conflict in the Countryside" Farmers Weekly, April 17 1981.

CHAPTER 9
AIR POLLUTION: A PROBLEM IN LAND USE

I.A. Nicholson
Institute of Terrestrial Ecology, Banchory

ABSTRACT

The author considers representative types of airborne pollutants and some of the
important atmospheric processes involved in their evolution and aerial distribution. The particular pollutant characteristics of areas influenced by towns and
cities are classified and attention concentrated on those conditions found where
the urban hinterland is a large area of mixed semi-rural countryside such as the
hinterland of Glasgow. Methods of evaluating damage to crop plants by air pollutants are discussed and the need for further research stated.

KEYWORDS

Urban hinterland; airborne pollutants; primary and secondary pollutants; area
sources; point sources; sulphur dioxide; acid rain; photochemical reactions;
ozone events; data sources; crop injury.

INTRODUCTION

In this paper air pollution and its importance in areas adjacent to cities is
considered primarily from the viewpoint of horticulture, agriculture and forestry.
The focus is mainly on conditions in Scotland where until recently atmospheric
pollution in relation to crop production has received little attention.

Following the theme of this symposium - Where the City Meets the Country - it might
seem logical to consider air pollution in a restricted context with a narrow and
perhaps arbitrary definition of the urban/rural interface. However, this would
preclude from discussion many problems in forestry and agriculture which must be
considered in a broader framework. Moreover the recognition that certain pollutants can travel large distances from emission sources establishes atmospheric
pollution as a regional, if not a global, phenomenon and it is therefore necessary
to recognise interface zones between cities and the countryside as parts of a
large-scale and complex spatial pattern.

AIRBORNE POLLUTANTS

Two broad types of pollutant source are recognised, namely 'point' sources and
'area' sources, the former often being located in relatively clean air areas and

include coal- or oil-burning power stations, smelters, brickworks and paper mills. In the vicinity of these sources ground-level pollutant concentrations character- istically show wide fluctuations in time, the patterns being strongly affected by speed and direction of the wind.

Area sources, represented by built up areas comprising domestic and industrial emissions, also contain major point sources. Typically, in these circumstances emission sources release pollutants at heights varying from a few metres to 100 m or more. A characteristic feature of an area source, by contrast to an isolated point source, is that the area source tends to produce a persistent 'base load' of pollutants in the atmosphere.

Polluted atmospheres comprise complex mixtures of gaseous and particulate substances, permeating at least to the level of the 'mixing height' limited vertically by a temperature inversion (Pasquill 1971). Pollutants also become incorporated in rain drops, causing changes in pH of rain. Substances present and their concentrations in the atmosphere are constantly changing according to source characteristics and the effectiveness of 'sinks' such as vegetation and soils, and also as a result of chemical reactions in the atmosphere itself.

Pollutants such as sulphur dioxide (SO_2) and hydrogen fluoride emitted directly from sources, for example smelter or power station chimneys, are known as primary pollutants. Secondary pollutants which arise from chemical reactions in the atmos- phere include ozone (O_3) and sulphates (e.g. H_2SO_4). As air masses age the pro- portion of secondary pollutants increases; for example, SO_2 is gradually oxidised to sulphate in the aerosol phase.

A simple classification of gaseous pollutants derived from fuel combustion and various industrial processes is shown in Table 9.1. Until recently the atmosphere in and around many cities contained large quantities of smoke, the decline in the past two decades being the most obvious benefit of the Clean Air Act (1956). Other particulates often present are fluorides, found especially around aluminium smelters and brickworks, and a range of heavy metals including lead released by car exhausts.

TABLE 9.1   Common Atmospheric Pollutants

Primary (Gaseous)	Secondary Derivatives

(1) From fuel combustion
      Carbon dioxide
      Carbon monoxide	

	PAN
Unburned Hydrocarbons ————————————	Oxone
	Other oxidants Acidity in
Oxides of nitrogen —————————————————	rainfall
Sulphur dioxide	
Aldehydes	

(2) From industrial processes
      Organic vapours
      Acids, acidic aerosols
      Aldehydes
      Fluorides, chlorides, bromides
      Hydrogen sulphide (oxidised to SO_2)	

Source: After Holdgate (1979).

It is not practicable to consider in detail each of the major groups of pollutants.
Discussion is therefore confined to SO_2, a primary pollutant, and ozone, a secondary pollutant, along with other substances closely associated with atmospheric
processes implicating these gases (Table 9.1).

                    SOME IMPORTANT ASMOSPHERIC PROCESSES

Not surprisingly, toxic effects on plants depend on the chemical forms in which
emitted pollutants occur and on the transformations taking place between emission
sources and the plant receptors. A brief survey of some important processes is
therefore appropriate.

Sulphur Dioxide: Chemical Changes and Deposition

Sulphur dioxide emitted from a chimney is diluted largely by atmospheric turbulence,
and becomes dispersed throughout the mixing layer. The gas is removed from the
lower atmosphere in the absence of rain by two main processes;

(i) dry deposition to foliage or other surfaces on the ground; and

(ii) transformation to sulphate by oxidation and hydration.

Dry deposition of SO_2 to vegetation takes place on external surfaces of plants, but
molecules also move into leaves through stomata. At the same time as deposition is
taking place the whole air parcel is moving according to the speed and direction of
the wind.

Transformation rates of SO_2 are affected by atmospheric conditions, including temperature, light and the presence of other pollutants: all these conditions can
change during transport, thus affecting the scale of gas transport. In certain
conditions (which include strong winds, stable atmosphere or low-level inversion
layer) relatively large distances can be covered. At Eindhoven in the Netherlands,
for example, easterly winds often produced large concentrations of SO_2 which was
apparently transported from the Ruhr, 100 km to the east (Zeedijk & Velds 1973).

Oxidation of SO_2 occurs in both gas- and liquid-phases. Gas-phase reactions are
strongly promoted by photochemical reactions which generate oxidants, but thermal
reactions are also important, especially when the presence of other pollutants
produces reactive intermediates that take part in the oxidation process. Liquid-
phase reactions are more important than the light-stimulated type in dull humid
conditions.

These transformation processes lead to the formation of acid rain, often hundreds
of km from gas sources. Raindrops may form round acidic condensation nuclei whereas
washout of gaseous SO_2 by descending rain may also increase rain acidity (Fowler
1980). Although sulphate is usually primarily associated with increased acidity
of rain, nitrate and chloride are also implicated.

Oxides of Nitrogen, Hydrocarbons and Ozone: Photochemical reactions

It is useful to consider these pollutants as a group because pollutant ozone is a
product of photochemical reactions involving oxides of nitrogen (NO_x) and reactive
hydrocarbons. All three substances, however, can themselves be phyto-toxic.

Ozone at the earth's surface is not altogether a product of reactions between
industrial precursors. It occurs naturally in the stratosphere at about 25 km above
the earth where it is generated by ultra-violet light dissociating molecular oxygen.
Although the importance of different O_3 sources contributing to background levels

is still uncertain (Fishman & Crutzen 1978), downward mixing appears to be an important natural source of O_3 causing large concentrations at the earth's surface in the spring and early summer. Substantial amounts of pollutant ozone along with other oxidants (e.g. peroxyacetylnitrate or PAN) are formed photochemically in the presence of NO_x, large quantities of which are produced by motor car exhausts, and unburnt hydrocarbons. Nitrogen dioxide occupies a position of special importance in this complex process: it is a light-absorber and triggers photochemical reactions. Meteorological conditions promoting these reactions are bright sunlight, high temperature and low wind speed, conditions found typically in anticyclonic conditions (Bell 1978).

Natural processes as well as man's activities are important sources of NO_x. Nitric oxide (NO) can be produced in large amounts by bacterial action whereas pollutant NO is formed during high-temperature combustion in air (though NO is not in itself a combustion product). Nitrogen dioxide (NO_2) is emitted as such but more commonly it occurs as a secondary pollutant, being formed in the atmosphere by NO oxidation.

In emissions from coal combustion and waste incineration 109 and 211 organic substances respectively have been identified, hydrocarbons being well represented (Junk and Ford 1980). Large amounts of hydrocarbons are produced naturally, the largest natural source of photochemically reactive hydrocarbons is thought to be tree foliage which releases terpenes. Large quantities of reactive hydrocarbons (including many gaseous olefins) are also emitted from industrial sources but it is noteworthy that, according to Rasmussen (1972), the natural production of terpenes is more than 6 times greater than man-made emissions of reactive olefins. Ethylene, a natural product as well as one of industrial origin, can have profound effects on plants, inhibiting growth and accelerating the ageing process.

POLLUTANT CHARACTERISTICS OF AREAS INFLUENCED BY TOWNS AND CITIES

Definition of Areas Affected

From the foregoing discussion it is clear that different atmospheric pollutants, especially if acid rain is included, show different spatial relationships with sources and affect areas around sources on different scales.

For present purposes it is convenient to recognise three main zones:

(i) a zone forming the immediate periphery of contiguous urban development, up to c. 2 km from the city boundary;

(ii) an urban hinterland up to, say, 50 km or more; and

(iii) remote areas.

It is difficult to generalise about air pollution in zone (i) because much depends on the particular 'mix' of sources in urban areas (Moss 1975) and on other circumstances such as local topography. On the other hand, remote areas or regional zones are too extensive for detailed treatment in this discussion. Zone (ii) is of special interest, links between city and country being fairly clearly recognised. It can be subdivided into two fairly distinct types:

(a) Conditions where the conurbation adjoins an extensive rural area in which the city's influence can be expected to diminish with increasing distance from the city, leading to distant areas with relatively clean air. An example might be Edinburgh and its hinterland extending in an easterly direction to the productive farm lands of East Lothian and beyond to the Lammermuir Hills (Fig. 9.1).

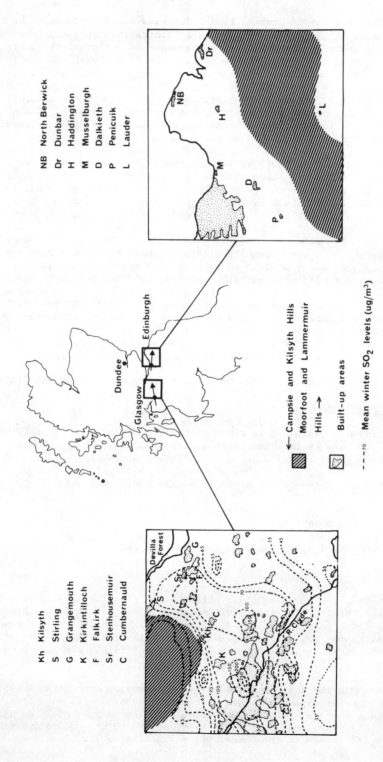

Fig. 9.1   AIR POLLUTION: HINTERLANDS OF GLASGOW AND EDINBURGH

(b) Conditions where the urban hinterland is broken up by numerous small towns
and/or point sources providing a large area of mised semi-rural countryside. An
example of this type is represented by the hinterland of Glasgow on the eastern
side of the city (Fig. 9.1).

This discussion will be concerned mainly with the latter type (Zone iib), the
hinterland of Glasgow extending eastwards into the Central Valley of Scotland
providing a useful practical example.

Gaseous Pollutants

Monitoring data on gas (mainly SO_2) concentrations in the Glasgow hinterland are
available from several sources, namely the National Survey (National Survey of Air
Pollution 1961-71, 1976-79), the Forth Valley Survey (Keddie, Bower, Mauchan,
Roberts and Williams 1978) and ITE's station near Kincardine-on-Forth (Devilla
Forest): these latter records are of special value because of the frequent measurements made not only for SO_2 but also for NO_x and O_3 (Nicholson, Fowler, Paterson,
Cape and Kinnaird 1980). Unfortunately, most monitoring stations are in built-up
areas, a notable exception being the ITE station. Additonal pollution data relating mainly to SO_2 are available from a lichen survey which covered both urban and
rural parts of the Glasgow hinterland (O'Hare 1974). Very few measurements of
hydrocarbons have been made, the limited data being of little value in the present
discussion.

(i)   Sulphur dioxide and oxides of nitrogen. O'Hare's lichen survey suggested
that most of the Glasgow hinterland was exposed to mean winter values exceeding
65 µg SO_2 m^{-3}, a central strip extending from Glasgow through the Cumbernauld Gap
being exposed to more than 100 µg m^{-3}. Figures from the Forth Valley Survey
(1973-76) (Keddie et al, 1978) suggested much lower concentrations in the eastern
part of the hinterland, possibly 35-45 µg SO_2 m^{-3} for much of the area except
around centres such as Falkirk and Grangemouth. Recent mean winter values for
some scattered locations east of Glasgow are shown in Table 9.2. Data from ITE's
station with an annual mean concentration of 30 µg SO_2 m^{-3} (winter mean concentrations about 30% higher), are in much closer agreement with values found by the
Forth and the National Surveys than with values suggested by O'Hare. Although the
map prepared by Fowler & Cape (1980) showing annual mean concentrations based on
OECD 1974 emission data for Scotland (Fig. 9.2) indicates values consistent with
the lichen data, and much higher values for the whole of the Central Valley than
those suggested by direct SO_2 measurements, the estimates are regarded as being
too high (Fowler & Cape, personal communication).

An important feature of O'Hare's data, collected in 1972, is that the distribution
of lichens was probably affected by historical factors and slow recolonisation by
these plants. In the 10 years from 1961 smoke concentrations in Scotland (at urban
sites) declined by 64% and SO_2 concentrations by 33%. Large percentage decreases
for two individual stations in the Central Valley are also shown in Table 9.2.
Data from another, more limited, lichen survey are in fact consistent with this
interpretation. Miller (1975) conducted a survey in Devilla Forest and interpreted
lichen distribution to suggest concentrations in the range 70-125 µg SO_2 m^{-3},values
much higher than those found more recently by ITE using gas measuring equipment.

Unfortunately, too few data on SO_2 concentrations are available for the area east
of Edinburgh (Fig. 9.1) to enable a detailed comparison to be made of the hinterlands of Glasgow and Edinburgh. However, ITE data for a station about 8 km from
the centre of Edinburgh indicate mean annual concentrations of about 16 µg SO_2 m^{-3},
suggesting very low values for rural parts of Midlothian and East Lothian.

TABLE 9.2   Mean Winter SO_2 Contrations (µg m^{-3}) in the Central Valley Eastwards from the Periphery of Glasgow.   Per Cent Decrease in SO_2 Concentrations and Smoke Shown for Two Stations with Long Runs of Data

	Mean winter SO_2 concentration[2] (µg m^{-3})	Per cent decrease			
		1966-67 to 1978-79		1962-63 to 1978-79	
		SO_2	Smoke	SO_2	Smoke
Glasgow periphery (Nr. Easterhouse)	84	30	72	–	–
Kirkintilloch	90	–	–	–	–
Kilsyth (1977-78, 1978-79)	54	–	–	–	–
Stirling County (Stenhousemuir)	45	–	–	70	88
Kincardine-on-Forth[1] (1976-77, 1978-79)	26	–	–	–	–

Source: Data from National Survey stations (National Survey of Air Pollution 1961-71 and 1976-79).
[1] Outside main are considered.
[2] Values averaged over 1976-77, 1977-78 and 1978-79 except where otherwise indicated.

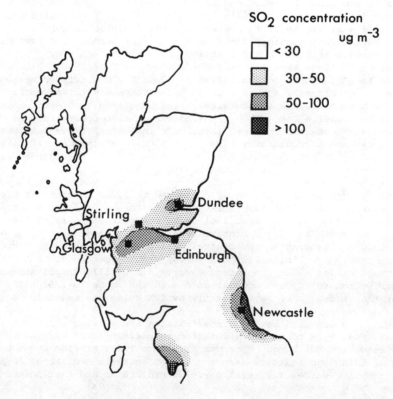

Fig. 9.2 SO_2 CONCENTRATION SCOTLAND AND NORTH ENGLAND

Few data are available for concentration of NO_x (NO and NO_2) in the area being considered. An indication of expected concentrations, however, can be taken from Fowler & Cape (1980) who quote a mass ratio of NO_2/SO_2 at rural stations of about 0.8.

Gas concentrations at Devilla Forest measured every 10 minutes during 1977-80 provide a more detailed understanding of exposure patterns of SO_2, NO_x and O_3 likely to be encountered in the more rural parts of the Central Valley (Nicholson, Fowler, Paterson, Cape and Kinnaird 1980). Fig. 9.3a shows the annual variation in concentrations, the dominant features being the occurrence of relatively small values during the summer and high values in the autumn and winter (due to fossil fuel combustion). Similarly a diurnal cycle occurs; peak (SO_2) concentrations occurring during the morning (Fig. 9.3b). Concentrations of NO_x show cycles similar to those of SO_2 on both annual and diurnal scales. Moreover SO_2 and NO_x/NO concentrations are positively correlated (SO_2/NO_x, $r = 0.58$; SO_2/NO, $r = 0.51$) suggesting that common sources of SO_2 and NO_x are probably involved. The peaks at about 0900 hours probably reflect the trapping of early morning emissions below the inversion layer.

(ii) <u>Ozone</u>. Pollution by ozone (and other oxidants) was thought for a long time to be associated with typical continental 'sunny' climates such as in California. In July 1971, however, elevated ozone levels were recorded in the south of England (Atkins, Cox & Eggleton 1972). In this part of the country polluted air carrying ozone or its precursors from areas of origin on the continent may be enriched in ozone by local photochemical activity causing periodic short-term episodes. It is now known that pollutant ozone occurs throughout the British Isles with the possible exception of northern Scotland (Ashmore, Bell & Reilly, 1978). Indirect evidence of the occurrence of ozone 'events' has recently been produced for West Central Scotland (Sweeney 1981). Indeed, direct measurements in the Central Valley by ITE have demonstrated the occurrence of photochemical (pollutant) ozone events.

The annual cycle of ozone concentrations at Devilla shows a marked peak during the spring and summer months (Fig. 9.3a). Although natural processes affect background levels in the annual cycle (10-40 ppb)* diurnal cycles are strongly influenced by photochemical activity involving air pollutants. The diurnal cycle has a distinct peak in the middle of the day: concentrations rise from very low levels early in the morning and return to similar levels during the evening and at night.

Over the country as a whole, the frequency of occurrence of 'events' during which concentrations exceed 50 ppb is of the order of 100 hours per year, though very variable, and the mean duration of a single event is about 6 hours, with a mean concentration of about 100 ppb. At Devilla such events occur on about 20 days each year (Fowler and Cape, 1980 (Fig. 9.3a, 9.3b). Data from Devilla, show that by contrast to SO_2 and NO_x, O_3 and NO_x are negatively correlated (O_3/NO_x, $r = -0.50$, O_3/NO, $r = 0.37$), presumably because of reactions between NO and O_3.

(iii) <u>Short-term fluctuations.</u> Measurements at Devilla Forest have shown that very large concentrations, especially of SO_2 and NO_x, occur for short periods lasting minutes or hours. These values are obscured by the 11-day running means used for the construction of Fig. 9.3a and the mean values shown in Fig. 9.3b. During a 5-day period in November/December 1977, for example, SO_2 concentrations exceeded 300 µg m^{-3} for several hours with higher peaks during shorter intervals, indeed levels of more than 350 µg SO_2 m^{-3} were recorded. Sulphur dioxide concentrations reached values 10 times greater than mean values, indicating how misleading mean values can be when considering effects on plants. Concentrations of NO_x also fluctuate strongly, the pattern often following closely that of SO_2.

 *(by volume)

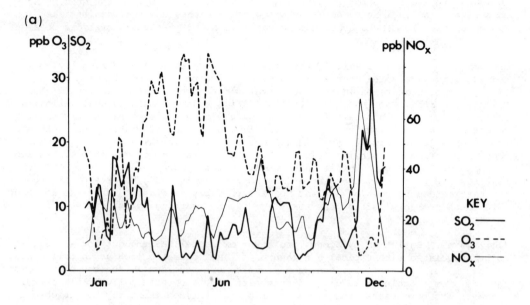

Fig. 9.3a   DEVILLA FOREST: ANNUAL CYCLE OF NO_x, O_3, SO_2 CONCENTRATIONS

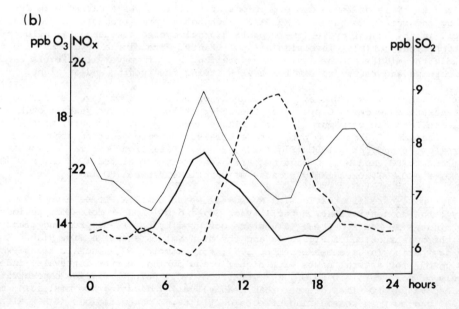

Fig. 9.3b   DEVILLA FOREST: SHORT TERM FLUCTUATIONS NO_x, O_3, SO_2

TABLE 9.3   Estimates of Time (%) that SO_2 Concentrations
will be Exceeded

Annual arithmetic mean ($\mu g\ m^{-3}$)	Concentration ($\mu g\ m^{-3}$)			
	50	100	200	300
<30	<11	<1.3	<0.06	<0.01
30-50	11-31	1.3-7.0	0.06-0.62	0.01-0.10
50-100	31-69	7.0-30	0.62-7.0	0.1 -1.8
>100	>69	>30	>7	>1.8

Source: Fowler & Cape (1980)

Using average annual values Fowler & Cape (1980) have estimated the fraction of
time that certain values are expected to be exceeded (Table 3). In the range of
30-50 $\mu g\ m^{-3}$ average annual concentration of SO_2, for example, 100 $\mu g\ SO_2\ m^{-3}$ may
be exceeded for 1.3 to 7.0% of the time. For NO_2 in the concentration range 25-40
$\mu g\ m^{-3}$ a concentration of 100 $\mu g\ m^{-3}$ would be exceeded for a very small percentage
of the time (0.01-0.05%) (Table 9.4).

TABLE 9.4   Estimates of Time (%) that NO_2 Concentrations
will be Exceeded

Annual arithmetic mean ($\mu g\ m^{-3}$)	Concentration ($\mu g\ m^{-3}$)			
	50	100	200	300
<25	<0.5	<0.01	-	-
25-40	0.5-12	0.01-0.05	0.01	-
40-80	12-80	0.05-11	0.01-0.8	0.05
>80	>80	>11	>0.8	>0.05

Source: Fowler & Cape (1980)

In addition to the occurrence of short-term 'peaks' of individual pollutants a most
important feature from the point of view of plant injury is the coincidence of high
values of at least two pollutants, a problem which is considered later.

Acid Rain

The regional character of rain acidity has already been emphasised and the role of
transformations in gaseous pollutants (SO_2, NO_x) during long-range transport has
been indicated. Rain acidity is mentioned in the present context largely for the
purpose of outlining background conditions in the zone which here is the main focus
of interest.

Taking Scotland as a whole, the regional character of rain acidity can be clearly recognised from ITE data. Acidity increases from west to east (Fig. 9.4), the Central Valley showing pH values of 4.4 to 4.5 in the west and 4.3 to 4.4 in the east. Local effects can also be identified, for example, in Glasgow itself rain pH has been predicted assuming the absence of pollutant emissions there. The actual and predicted values were pH 4.3 and 4.4 respectively. This difference may be accounted for, in part, by the effect of SO_2 washout from the atmosphere increasing the acidity of descending rain drops (Fowler 1980). It is worth noting that rain acidity is not always greater in cities than in areas further afield, indeed a reverse relationship may occur (Moss 1975).

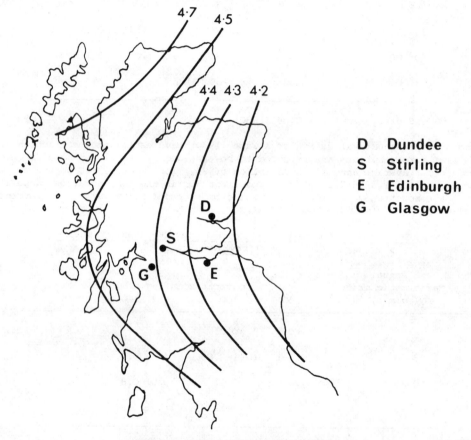

Fig. 9.4   RAIN ACIDITY, SCOTLAND

PROBLEMS OF CROP INJURY

Many studies on effects of airborne pollutants in crop plants grown in horticulture and forestry have been done in the USA and in Europe. For British conditions there are still insufficient data to enable a rigorous evaluation to be made of field effects of airborne pollutants on crops. However, a general discussion based on selected published reports, many of only indirect relevance, may help to clarify the particular circumstances of the Central Valley.

Lichen Indicators

Lichens vary greatly in tolerance to air pollutants. Data on lichen distribution

can therefore be useful in helping to interpret pollution conditions, although
observations on lichens are no substitute for studies directly applicable to
economic crops. In a study of the western part of the Central Valley, O'Hare (1974)
showed that for three species (Hypogymnia physodes, Evernia prunastri and Usnea
subfloridana) the so-called 'desert' zone where the species were absent extended
over a large area beyond the Glasgow conurbation. Supporting studies strongly
indicated that the lichen data reflected mean SO_2 concentrations rather than other
factors and, taken together, the three species defined a belt bounded approximately
by the 45 and 65 µg SO_2 m^{-3} mean winter isopleths. In an easterly direction the
desert edge encompassed much of the Glasgow hinterland discussed in this account
and included the edge of the Campsie Fells and Kilsyth Hills (Fig. 9.1).

Crop Plants

Observations in Europe and North America suggest that the more susceptible coniferous
species to SO_2 pollution include Scots pine (Pinus sylvestris), Norway spruce (Picea
abies), sitka spruce (P. sitchensis) and eastern white pine (Pinus strobus). Amongst
deciduous species, grey alder (Alnus incana), hazel (Corylus avellana) and rowan
(Sorbus aucuparia) are relatively susceptible and some reports include silver birch
(Betula pendula).

In the Glasgow hinterland adverse effects of air pollution on commercial timber trees
have been suspected for a long time. At the forests of Lennox and Cumbernauld the
poor growth of sitka spruce in particular was thought to be associated with air
pollution. Records from lead dioxide gauges in the early 1960s suggested that SO_2
pollution was at a comparable level, at least at Cumbernauld, to the less severely
polluted stations in the Pennines (Davies 1968), where air pollution was thought
to be adversely affecting tree growth.

The complexities in assessing field responses to air pollutants were emphasised by
Lines (1979) reporting the performance of 26 different tree species planted between
1951 and 1977 on a variety of sites in the southern Pennines. Atmospheric pollution was measured with the lead dioxide candle method, sulphation rates in the early
years of this period suggesting that SO_2 pollution was comparable with pollution
conditions on the outskirts of nearby towns. Earlier plantings in the 1930s showed
particularly slow growth and heavy losses. By the late 1960s and early 1970s SO_2
concentrations had decreased. Maps published in 1975 (Gooriah, Keddie and Williams),
based on measured SO_2 concentrations indicated mean winter concentrations in the
area of no more than 90 µg SO_2 m^{-3}.

Responses to atmospheric pollutants in these field experiments were obscured by
other factors affecting tree performance such as soil conditions and cultural treat-
ments. No doubt growth was also considerably affected by the smoke pollution which
was formerly widespread. Sitka spruce which was widely used showed disappointing
growth on sites that in unpolluted areas would have given expectations of good
growth. However, growth improved dramatically after canopy closure. Scots pine
grew poorly whereas sycamore (Acer pseudoplatanus), although difficult to establish
and slow to grow, was one of the few species found growing healthily to a large
size in the area. Silver birch showed a high degree of tolerance.

The poor performance of Scots pine in the industrial Pennines was linked with air
pollution over an extensive area (Farrer, Relton and Rutter 1977). Occurrence in
10 km grid squares was strongly correlated with mean winter SO_2 concentrations
though values compared with the Glasgow hinterland were high, up to over 250 µg
SO_2 m^{-3}. Controlled experiments have also demonstrated the sensitivity of Scots
pine to SO_2. Exposure of 3-year old pine (growing in chambers) to a mean concentration of 143 µg SO_2 m^{-3} during 18 months caused accelerated senescence and
decreased Relative Growth Rate by 14% compared with the filtered air treatment

(Garsed, Rutter & Relton 1981).   Similar studies with birch (B. pendula and B. pubescens), sycamore and oak(Quercus robur) indicated that these broadleaved species are more tolerant of prolonged exposure to SO_2 than is Scots pine (Garsed, Farrar and Rutter 1979).

The available data do not enable SO_2 effects on trees to be evaluated in the Glasgow hinterland where much of the area is exposed to annual average SO_2 concentrations less than the 50-100 μg m^{-3} range.   Understanding of plant processes, however, does suggest that some impairment of growth mechanisms may be expected in parts of the area, particularly in view of the occurrence of short-term surges of SO_2 and NO_x which often coincide.   The only direct field evidence suggesting pollutant stress in the Glasgow hinterland is the occurrence of premature loss of needles in Scots pine, though this has not been correlated with growth.

Agricultural and horticultural crops suggested by overseas authors to be relatively susceptible to SO_2 pollution include oats, barley, wheat lucerne, turnip, Brussels sprouts, lettuce, radish and gooseberry (Jeffree 1976).   However, studies in Britain have not covered a sufficient number of species to permit ranking with regard to SO_2 sensitivity.

The most intensively studied agricultural crop plant in Britain in relation to air pollution is perennial ryegrass (Lolium perenne).In 1952 Bleasdale (1973), working in an area of coal-smoke pollution, showed that growth of S23 ryegrass in glass- house experiments was improved when plants were supplied with filtered air.   Sub- sequent work showed that continuous exposure to SO_2 could cause growth impairment without producing visible leaf injury (Lockyer, Cowling and Jones 1976) and the populations of ryegrass long-exposed to polluted atmospheres developed tolerances to SO_2 (Bell & Mudd 1976).   Although many experiments have been done with S23 (a relatively susceptible cultivar) to determine responses to SO_2, results have been conflicting.   Bell et al. (1979) suggested that as a generalisation decreased growth in summer could be expected at mean concentrations of 100 to 150 μg SO_2 m^{-3}.   Never- theless some results obtained by these authors indicated that concentrations of less than 50 μg SO_2 m^{-3} substantially impaired growth.   Slow growth is thought to increase the potential for SO_2 toxicity.

In experiments with barley (var. Abacus) in chambers receiving filtered and unfil- tered ambient air, mean grain yields with filtered air were almost double those supplied with unfiltered air.   This study was situated in an area of Bedfordshire affected by emission from brickworks, mean growing season concentrations of SO_2 being 61 μg m^{-3}.   However, fluoride was also present (0.8 μg m^{-3}), the results with barely no doubt being a result of interactive effects of the two pollutants (Brough, Parry and Whittingham 1978).

Evidence for SO_2 injury to field-grown horticultural crops in Britain is sparse. Laboratory studies have shown that net photosynthesis in field bean (Vicia faba) can be decreased (relative to clean air) at SO_2 concentrations of about 100 μg m^{-3}, but growth responses under field conditions have not yet been established. (Black and Unsworth 1979).   Similarly, in glasshouse crops there is lttle evidence of SO_2 injury caused by pollution of the outside atmosphere: the effect of the external atmosphere is thought to be small since the influx of air is usually slow (Ashenden, Mansfield & Harrison 1977).

There is little direct field evidence in Britain suggesting that at ambient levels the other primary pollutants being considered here injure crop plants.   However laboratory fumigations of tomato (Lycopersicon esculentum)with NO_2 have produced decisive effects, for example, concentrations of 500 μg NO_2 m^{-3} throughout the growing period decreased yield by 22% (Spierings 1971).   With glasshouse crops the burning of fossil fuels for heating and to provide CO_2 enrichment can also

produce toxic amounts of nitrogen oxides and unburnt hydrocarbons, especially
ethylene.

Pollution by elevated ozone concentrations causes widespread economic damage to
crops in North America. Although not strictly relevant to crop production problems
in Britain, it is salutary to note that recent studies with a highly sensitive
variety of tobacco (Nicotiana tabacum), grown as a test species throughout the UK,
showed that leaf injury occurred over most of the country (Ashmore, Bell and Reily
1978). Injury to commercial crop species was first observed in the field (Southern
England) in 1978 when mean hourly concentrations exceeded 0.10 ppm for several days:
foliar lesions were found on pea (Pisum sativum) and radish (Raphanus sativus) and
some evidence of ozone injury was also found in maize (Zea mays) and tomato (Ashmore,
Bell, Dalpra and Runeckles 1980). Another species thought to show symptoms is
spinach (Spinacia oleracea). Controlled experiments with potato (Solanum tuberosum)
and other crop plants suggest that leaf injury symptoms can be expected to occur at
ambient O_3 concentrations experienced in Britain (see Bell 1978).

Atmospheric pollutants present in mixtures are often more injurious to plants than
when they occur singly. Controlled experiments on various plants have demonstrated
enhanced effects, sometimes synergistic, for example; effects of SO_2 and NO_2 on
radish (Bennet, Hill, Soleimani & Edwards 1975), lucerne (Medicago sativa)(White,
Hill & Bennet 1974) and several grass species (Ashenden 1979; Ashenden and Williams
1980). The serious disease chloratic dwarf of white pine in the USA is caused by
the presence of both O_3 and SO_2. No similar effects on trees in Britain have been
reported but net photosynthesis in field beans which is depressed by SO_2 at concentrations commonly occurring in Britain is still further depressed by superimposing
O_3 at concentrations found in the field under photochemical conditions. The effect
would be particularly marked near urban areas where sources of the appropriate
pollutants and precursors are most frequent (Ormrod, Black & Unsworth 1981).

        EVALUATION

Available evidence does not indicate that serious economic damage to crop plants
in forestry, agriculture and horticulture is widespread today in the Glasgow Hinterland (Zone 11b). If damage is occurring it is likely to be less serious in the case
of SO_2 (and smoke) than before the Clean Air Acts were introduced. However, it
would be naive to conclude that air pollution in the Glasgow hinterland is econ-
omically unimportant.

It is salutary to recall that as a result of improved research methods over the
last 50 years, there has been a progressive decrease in SO_2 concentrations thought
to represent threshold values for plant injury. In relation to the 'higher' plants
the evolution of ideas has been clearly expressed by Tamm and Aronsson (1972):
"About 1900 and for some time later, it was believed that 5700 µg m^{-3} was the limit
at which damage might occur. About 1950, the threshold value was considered to be
570 µg m^{-3} but now, 20 years later, it is more likely to be 57 µg m^{-3} if measured
as an arithmetic mean value. It is still not possible to determine a threshold
value below which no damage may occur".

Knowledge of processes within plants affected by air pollutants has increased
greatly in recent years, but few studies have so far been able to show how and to
what extent these biochemical and physiological responses are expressed in crop
growth and 'quality', nor has it been shown what significance short-term high
concentrations may have under field conditions. Similarly, laboratory studies on
whole plants have led to great advances in understanding the effects of pollutant
mixtures on growth but understanding of field conditions is still very limited.
Other effects that are just beginning to be studied are concerned with reproduction and the relationship between crop plants, pest attack and disease

occurrence. Much is still to be learnt about the importance of stress caused by
gaseous air pollutants and possibly by acid rain, when superimposed on natural
environmental stresses.

As regards secondary pollutants in the Glasgow hinterland, conditions may be more
suitable than formerly for O_3 formation owing to the clearer atmosphere. The
existence of conditions suitable for photochemical reactions emphasises the need
to bear in mind changes in concentrations of precursors, namely NO_x and hydrocarbons,
that may arise from new industrial ventures. Experience elsewhere suggests that
freedom from ozone damage cannot be assumed.

It must be emphasised that although none of the reports considered in this account
give any direct indication of the pollutant stresses to which crop plants are
exposed in the Glasgow hinterland, they are of considerable importance in several
respects namely:

(i) in illustrating that evidence for pollutant injury to crops is widespread,

(ii) in demonstrating that effects have been reported in the SO_2 and O_3 concentration ranges found, or to be expected in the Glasgow hinterland, at least during
short-term 'peaks', and

(iii) in drawing attention to the occurrence of enhanced, sometimes synergistic,
effects involving pollutant mixtures applied to a range of plants in controlled
experiments and hence the need for constant alertness to potential hazards in the
field.

The recognition that gaseous air pollutants can adversely affect growth in the
absence of visual symptoms of plant injury accentuates the importance of understanding how plants respond to small foses of air pollutants. These may insidi-
ously undermine attempts to improve the efficiency of production systems.

Finally, having drawn attention to the need for caution in anticipating pollutant
effects on crop plants in zone (ii) defined as the Glasgow hinterland, it is
equally important to emphasise that in zone (i), the peripheral zone round Glasgow,
an area not considered in detail in this paper, pollutant stresses to which plants
are exposed are likely to be much more severe. Indeed, in the absence of further
data there must be a strong presumption that the 'performance' of some crop species
growing there is distinctly impaired.

ACKNOWLEDGMENTS

I wish to thank my colleagues Dr. J.N. Cape, Dr. D. Fowler, Mr. J. Kinnaird, and
Mr. I. S. Paterson for their helpful comments on the draft and Mr. I.S. Paterson
and Miss M. McPherson for preparation of the figures.

REFERENCES

Ashenden, T.W. 1979. The effect of long-term exposures to SO_2 and NO_2 pollution on
    the growth of Dactylis Glomerata L. and Poa pratensis L. Environ.Pollut.
    18, pp. 249-258.
Ashenden, T.W., Mansfield, T.A. & Harrison, R.M. 1977. Generation of air pollutants
    from kerosene combustion in commercial and domestic glasshouses. Environ.
    Pollut. 14, pp.93-100.
Ashenden, T.W. & Williams, I.A.D. 1980. Growth reductions in Lolium multiflorum
    Lam and Phleum pratense L. as a result of SO_2 and NO_2 pollution Environ.
    Pollut.(Ser. A.) 21, pp.131-139.

Ashmore, M.R., Bell, J.N.B., Dalpra, C. & Runeckles, V.C. 1980. Visible injury to crop species by ozone in the United Kingdom. Environ. Pollut. (Ser. A) .21, pp. 209-215.

Ashmore, M.R., Bell, J.N.B. & Reily, C.L. 1978. A survey of ozone levels in the British Isles using indicator plants. Nature, Lond. 276, pp.813-815.

Atkins, D.H.F., Cox, R.A. & Eggleton, A.E.J. 1972. Photochemical ozone and sulphuric acid aerosol formation in the atmosphere over southern England. Nature, Lond. 235, pp.372-376.

Bell, J.N.B. 1978. Ozone in the environment. Environmental Review: 6. Biologist. 25, pp.279-287.

Bell, J.N.B. & Mudd, C.H. 1976. Sulphur dioxide resistance in plants: a case study of Lolium perenne. In: Effects of Air pollutants on Plants. Ed. T.A. Mansfield, pp. 87-103. Cambridge Univ. Press.

Bell, J.N.B., Rutter, A.J. & Relton, J. 1979. Studies on the effects of low levels of sulphur dioxide on the growth of Lolium perenne L. New Phytol. 83, pp. 637-643.

Black, V.J. & Unsworth, M.H. 1979. Effects of low concentrations of sulphur dioxide on net photosynthesis and bark respiration of Vicia faba. J. Exp. Bot. 30, pp. 473-483.

Bleasdale, J.K.A. 1973. Effects of coal-smoke pollution gases on the growth of ryegrass (Lolium perenne L.) Environ Pollut. 5, pp.275-285.

Bennet, J.H., Hill, A.C. Soleimani, A. & Edwards, W.H. 1975. Acute effects of combination of sulphur dioxide and nitrogen dioxide on plants. Environ. Pollut. 9, pp. 127-132.

Brough, A., Parry, M.A. & Whittingham, C.P. 1978. The influence of aerial pollution on crop growth. Chem. Ind. No. 2, pp. 51-53.

Davies, E.J.M. 1968. Cumbernauld Forest. Scott. For. 22, pp. 228-234.

Farrer, J.F., Relton, J. & Rutter, A.J. 1977. Sulphur dioxide and the scarcity of Pinus sylvestris in the industrial Pennines. Environ. Pollut. 14, 63-38.

Fishman, J. & Crutzen, P.J. 1978. The origin of ozone in the troposphere. Nature, Lond. 274, pp. 855-858.

Fowler, D. 1980. Removal of sulphur and nitrogen compounds from the atmosphere in rain and by dry deposition. In: Ecological Impact of Acid Precipitation. Proceedings of International Conference, Norway. Eds. D. Drablos and A. Tollan pp. 22-32. SNSF Project As-NLH, Norway.

Fowler, D. & Cape, J.N. 1980. Air pollutants in agriculture and horticulture, Paper presented to 32nd School in Agricultural Science, Nottingham University.

Garsed, S.G., Farrar, J.F. & Rutter, A.J. 1979. The effects of low concentrations of sulphur dioxide on the growth of four broadleaved tree species. J. appl. Ecol. 16, 217-226.

Garsed, S.G., Rutter, A.J. & Relton, J. 1981. The effects of sulphur dioxide on the growth of Pinus sylvestris in two soils. Environ. Pollut. (Ser.A). 24, pp.219-232.

Gooriah, B.D., Keddie, A.W.C., & Williams, F.P. 1975. Smoke and SO_2 Contour maps of the U.K. Paper SCCB 85/4. Warren Spring Laboratory, 7 pp.

Holdgate, M.W. 1979. A Perspective of Environmental Pollution,Cambridge University Press.

Jeffree, C.E. 1976. Costs of sulphur dioxide to vegetation: a further study. University of Edinburgh, Department of Forestry and Natural Resources. pp. 1-80.

Junk, G.A. & Ford, C.S. 1980. A review of organic emissions from selected combustion processes. Chemosphere. 9, pp. 187-230.

Keddie, A.W.C., Bower, J.S., Maughan, G.H. & Williams, F.P. 1978. The Measurement, Assessment and Prediction of Air Pollution in the Forth Valley of Scotland - Final Report Warren Spring Laboratory, Stevenage.

Lines, R. 1979.   Performance of different species and seed origins in the industrial Pennines of Northern Britain. Paper presented to the IUFRO symposium, Poland.

Lockyer, D.R., Cowling, D.W. & Jones, L.H.P. (1976).   A system of exposing plants to atmospheres containing low concentrations of sulphur dioxide. J. exp. Bot. 27, pp. 397-409.

Miller, R.O. 1975. A report on Carron Valley Forest and Devilla Forest - Scotland: an assessment of SO$_2$ pollution using lichens as biological indicators. Internal Report, Institute of Terrestrial Ecology, Bangor.

Moss, M.R. 1975. Spatial patterns of precipitation reaction. Environ. Pollut. 8, pp. 301-315.

National Survey of Air Pollution 1961-71. HMSO, Lond.

National Survey of Air Pollution 1976-79. Annual Reports, Warren Spring Laboratory.

Nicholson, I.A., Fowler, D., Paterson, I.S., Cape, J.N., & Kinnaird, J.W. 1980. Continuous monitoring of airborne pollutants. In: Ecological Impact of Acid Precipitation, Proceedings of International Conference, Norway. Eds. D. Drablos and A. Tollan, pp. 144-145. SNSF Project As-NLH, Norway.

O'Hare, G.P. 1974.   Lichens and bark acidification as indicators of air pollution in west central Scotland. J. Biogeogr. 1, pp. 135-146.

Ormrod, D.P., Black, V.J., & Unsworth, M.V. 1981.   Depression of net photosynthesis in Vicia faba L. Exposed to sulphur dioxide and ozone. Nature, Lond. 291, pp. 585-586.

Pasquill, F. 1971.   Meteorological aspect of local high-concentration air pollution. In: Meteorology as Related to the Human Environment. pp. 49-54. WMO Special Environ. Rep. No. 2.

Rasmussen, R.A. 1972.   What do the hydrocarbons from trees contribute to air pollution? J. Air Pollut. Control Ass. 22, pp. 537-543.

Spierings, F.H.F.G. 1971. Influence of fumigations with NO$_2$ on growth and yield of tomato plants. Neth. J. Pl. Path. 77, pp. 194-200.

Sweeney, J.C. 1981.   Photochemical air pollution comes to central Scotland. Scott. Geogr. Mag. 97, pp. 50-56.

Tamm, C.O. & Aronsson, A. 1972. Research Notes (Royal College of Forestry), Department of Forest Ecology) No. 12, pp. 1-53.

White, K.L., Hill, A.C. & Bennet, J.H. 1974.   Synergestic inhibition of different photosynthesis rates by combinations of sulphur dioxide and nitrogen dioxide. Environ. Sci. & Technol. 8, pp. 574-576.

Zeedijk, H. & Velds, C.A. 1973.   The transport of sulphur dioxide over long distance. Atmos. Environ. 7, pp. 849-867.

COMMENT ON CHAPTERS 6, 7, 8 and 9 BY SYMPOSIUM DISCUSSANT

Eric C. Todd
The East of Scotland College of Agriculture

The Royal Scottish Geographical Society of Scotland and the University of Glasgow
Department of Geography are to be congratulated on bringing together such a variety
of parties with an interest in the interface between urban and rural areas.   In
the wide range of interests is seen part of the problem bedeviling this no-man's
land.

The country and the land user are faced with a two-fold problem, namely the direct
loss of high quality land and the indirect losses caused by the urban population.
Mr. Mackay rightly points out the scarcity and the location of prime quality land
in Scotland. What is more disturbing is the continuing high percentage, over 50
per cent, going for development. The higher percentage loss of prime land in the
Central Belt is most worrying. A misconception which often arises is with regard
to the present and potential use of such land. The Macaulay Institute classification is based upon the potential of the land rather than on its present use in
agriculture.

In respect of the indirect losses these give rise for more concern. It is to a
frugal Scottish instinct, a crying shame to see high quality land not expressing
its full potential in productive agriculture or forestry. Several reports including the NEDO Report on Land Use highlight this aspect. All the speakers in
their various ways cover most of the problems encountered by land users in the
urban fringe. Mr. Nicholson's contribution on air pollution adds a further hazard
to those already well recognised. One factor not mentioned directly but of significance is the very considerable additional insurances land users in such areas must
bear. A further difficulty experienced by land users is stress, which was highlighted by Mr. Mackay this morning.

With all the surveys that have been carried out in such diverse locations as Slough/
Hillingdon, Hertfordshire, Tyne & Wear, the Bollin Valley and Glenrothes one would
have thought that we would have learned some lessons. Unfortunately this is not
the case. In several of our new towns we are continuing to perpetuate and even
accentuate the problems encountered by land users on the urban fringe. The bad
planning referred to by the speakers often results in an increase in trespass which
in 80 per cent of cases leads to damage.

The way in which each contributor keeps very much to his own field rather than
accepting the need for a multi-disciplinary approach which may be more in tune with

95

the desires and aspiration of local people is a matter for concern. Mr. Mackay states that green-belts are "strictly speaking outside the Department's remit". Mr. Ross suggests that the public be encouraged to use "true rural situations for walking and recreation, preferably hill land". Mr. Jeffrey is of the opinion that "the execution of forest policy here is the province of the other National Agencies, Local Authorities and private enterprise rather than the Enterprise arm of the Forestry Commission". These are the easy options which lead for the most part to inaction and to an increase in the severity of the problems.

Of far more importance is a positive attitude. It is pleasing to note Mr. Jeffrey's comments about the Central Scotland Woodlands Project. Those parts of this scheme which, particularly, auger well for the future are the project officer's willingness to involve local people and to cross technical disciplines in seeking solutions to specific problems.

It is only through breaking out of our planning, agricultural and forestry compartments that we shall make some contribution to the solution of the vexed problems of the urban fringe. Often such an approach elucidates many exciting opportunities. In a small way the ESCA is attempting this. In conjunction with Countryside Commission of Scotland the ESCA initiated the Family Day on the Farm concept to inform the public of commercial agriculture. Through a job creation scheme ESCA produced a series of tape/slide presentations on modern agricultural topics for use in schools. Within the last few months ESCA has commenced the scheme whereby school teachers in Lothian Region after a short familiarisation course can conduct their own classes round a specific route on Langhill Dairy Farm. With Bush Estate being almost an oasis within the urban areas of Midlothian District the College is exploring ways of tackling the numerous difficulties and opportunities this presents. Another way in which ESCA is contributing to a solution of the problem is by taking part in courses for landscape and town and country planners at Edinburgh and Heriot-Watt Universities.

The more one examines the problems in the urban fringe the more one realises that they do not present insurmountable technical difficulties. However, they give rise to human ones. In essence the human conflicts are generally ones of communication between apparently diametrically opposed interests. Thus a plea, that the various disciplines and the local people make a joint effort to solve the problems and to take advantage of the opportunities presented.

CHAPTER 10

UNUSED LAND ON THE URBAN FRINGE IN SCOTLAND

Andrew H. Dawson
University of St. Andrews

ABSTRACT

The paper begins with a review of the theory of the effects of urban areas on
adjoining, but as yet undeveloped, land, and of the findings of some studies of
such land in this country and abroad. It notes the history of attempts to plan
the expansion of settlements and to protect rural land around them in the U.K.
Results of surveys made during the spring of 1981 of the use of land around the
edge of the built-up area of Edinburgh, Glenrothes and Perth are presented, together
with comparisons based on the Second Land Utilisation Survey. The extent of unused
and underused land there is compared with sample rural areas at a distance from
rural settlements. The distribution of unused land is related to the expected
pattern of future urban growth and to its capability for agricultural production.
The paper concludes with an assessment of the effectiveness of planning in this
country in the light of these results.

KEYWORDS

'idling' of land; a model of urban fringe land use; land market; measurement of
unused land; farmland losses to development; planning implications.

THE PROBLEM

Many writers have suggested that cities, by their very nature, cause land to fall
out of use. Several studies have demonstrated that there is much land at or beyond
the perimeter of urban settlements which formerly was used productively, but which
has since been abandoned. Such land is not in cultivation, nor does it show signs
of recent use as pasture, nor is it being used for recreation in an organised and
official manner, and it is not being developed. Some of it is dormant and some
derelict. It has been in use in the past, but has ceased to be used, and its output is being lost. Taken at their face value these studies must be alarming to
any society or government, such as those in post-war Britain, which believes that
it suffers from a shortage of land; and they must be doubly alarming in a country
in which the major urban settlements are, by and large, on or near the more fertile
soils. However, it would be quite wrong to accept either their findings or the
conclusions which have been drawn from them without careful examination of their
theoretical basis or of the evidence for them.

97

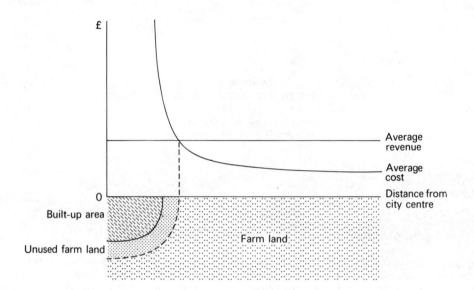

Fig. 10.1   A MODEL OF LAND USE AROUND A CITY

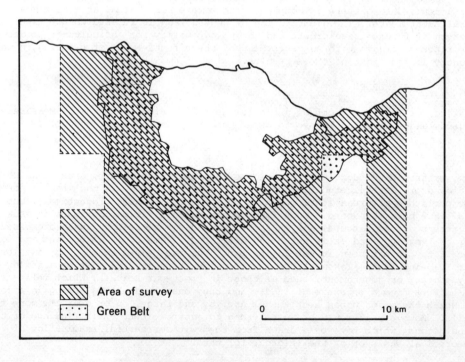

Fig. 10.2   AREA OF SURVEY AROUND EDINBURGH

A wide variety of reasons has been given for the "idling" of land, as it is sometimes called, around cities. Agriculture may be discouraged where there is frequent
trespass and damage to crops and property by neighbouring urban populations, or
where those populations try to stop farming practices which they consider to be
"noisome", such as the spreading of manure or crop dusting or the burning of stubble.
Land holdings may be fragmented by the construction of lines of communication into
cities, thus creating or isolating small parcels which in consequence become difficult to use. Atmospheric pollution from the urban area may accelerate the leaching
of soils and reduce crop yields; and, where tax is levied on land values, increasing burdens may fall on holdings close to the city edge which are becoming ripe
for development. Furthermore, farm-workers may take better-paid jobs in the city,
and farmers may lose interest in cultivation, pursue policies of under-capitalisa-
tion or "farming to quit", and land may deteriorate to the point at which further
production is not worthwhile.

A MODEL OF URBAN FRINGE LAND USE

This catalogue of malign influences may be expressed more succinctly by Fig. 10.1.
This shows some relationships between the returns to farmers, their costs of
production, and the consequent land-use effects. The average revenue curve indicates what the farmer may expect to receive as the price for a unit of his product.
In land-use theory of the von Thünen type this would decline with distance from the
city, but in today's conditions of agricultural marketing and transport in developed
countries it is likely that farm-gate prices will be fairly constant over wide
areas. The average cost of producing the unit, in contrast, is likely to rise very
rapidly at or close to the edge of the built-up area because of the increased
expenses of the sorts listed above or because constant overheads must still be paid
out of a yield which is reduced by damage, theft or the other consequences arising
out of proximity to the urban area. However, where rural activities and urban
development are allowed to compete freely, the chief reason for the rise in costs
will be the much higher rent levels which urban uses can command. Under perfect
competition equilibrium would be achieved when the urban area had expanded until
the rent for the last developed plot was just in excess of the highest payment that
any rural use could afford to make for it, and the interaction of the average cost
and revenue curves would occur at the boundary of the built-up area. However,
imperfections in the market make this unlikely. Land owners may not know exactly
what rent levels are available to them, and land may not be released for development exactly at the moment when higher rents could be obtained. Local government
control over the zoning of land may delay or prevent its development, and land
owners may not be willing to sell parcels of the size or shape required by developers. If the cost and revenue curves intersect at the edge of the built-up area
there will be no incentive to farmers to abandon production in advance of urban
development. If, on the other hand, intersection occurs before the built-up area
is reached, the intervening land will fall out of use.

How broad the zone of unused land will be at any moment will depend upon many
conditions affecting the land users. For example, any increase in the population
or economic activity of the built-up area is likely to increase the demand for
land from developers and so to raise the average cost curve and push the point of
intersection away from the edge of the built-up area. Conversely, any support for
agriculture in the form of guaranteed prices will raise the revenue curve and push
the point of intersection nearer to the city.   However, the cost curve is
usually rising so steeply at the boundary of the built-up area that only exceptional
increases in agricultural prices could cause the edge of the built-up area to
retreat and the return of developed land to rural uses. Indeed, developed land
which has been returned to agriculture or forestry has almost always been abandoned
and become derelict first; the arguments for its reclamation have been aesthetic

as well as economic, and such reclamation has been achieved usually with the help of government funds, that is, by the lowering of the cost curve, rather than in response to any increase in agricultural prices.

Fig. 10.1 gives the impression that a clear-cut zonation of land use will exist in the urban fringe, but this is improbable. Variations in the fertility of soils, in the suitability of land for development, in its accessibility to the dep- redations of the urban population and in the degree to which it is fragmented will give rise to a patchwork of parcels, some of which will suffer from above average costs, and will be more likely to go out of cultivation, and some which will enjoy relatively low costs of production and thus will tend to remain in rural uses. In these circumstances it may be difficult to observe the degree to which cities cause land to be unused, and to compare different urban hinterlands in this respect. Nevertheless, it is to such observations that we must turn because it is on the basis of these, rather than any theoretical models, that recent demands for govern- ment action to control land use in the urban fringe have been based.

SOME STUDIES OF UNUSED LAND IN THE URBAN FRINGE

Studies of dormant land in the urban fringe have been published over the last forty years, and many of those before 1974 have been reviewed by Munton. More recently high rates of idling have been reported from urban fringes in both the U.S.A. and the U.K. Berry recorded a rate of land idling caused by urban influ- ences of half a hectare for every hectare of development in a limited area of the Philadelphia Metropolitan Region between 1930 and 1970, and Coughlin and Berry showed that this had accelerated to one hectare in Chester county, Philadelphia between 1965 and 1975. More generally, the U.S. Department of Commerce reported that between 1967 and 1975 over one million hectares of farmland in the U.S.A. were developed each year, and that for every hectare so used another was idled by the effect of non-contiguous leapfrog development. In the U.K. the Greater London Council reported that in the borough of Hillingdon in 1971 an area equival- ent to about a quarter of the agricultural land was vacant (Low 1973), while Coleman showed that the amount of unused land in 851 km^2 of urban fringe around the Thames Estuary had doubled between 1962 and 1972 and occupied 9.3 percent of the total by the latter year. She also reported increasing rates of idling from the urban fringes of Merseyside and Surrey. Most recently Smith has reported that large areas of farm land around settlements in the Grampian Region and the Moray Firth have been "blighted".

Unfortunately these findings are difficult to interpret, because there is no common methodology amongst them, and it is not clear whether all employed a similar definition of unused land. Indeed, Coppock has drawn attention to the considerable difficulty which exists in establishing whether land is unused or not. All the studies imply, but do not demonstrate, that the rate of idling is higher in the urban fringe than elsewhere in rural areas with similar physical environments. However, if there is a marked spatial variation in the incidence of idling, the rates which have been calculated will be dependent upon the bound- ary of the urban fringe which has been adopted. In fact there is no agreed bound- ary, and the definitions of the urban fringe which have been offered by Coleman, Leeming and Sousson, and others are incapable of producing unambiguous lines on maps. Examination of the studies which have been cited suggests that their choices of boundary have been arbitrary. Furthermore, the studies by the G.L.C. and Coleman fail to distinguish between idling caused by proximity to large urban settlements and that caused by secular changes affecting rural activities through- out the country.

THE RESPONSE OF GOVERNMENT

Notwithstanding these problems, governments in both the U.S.A. and the U.K., and
in many other countries, have taken substantial powers to protect the countryside
from undesirable changes, and, in particular, to protect the areas around cities.
In this country the emphasis from the time of the Restriction of Ribbon Development
Act 1935 until the mid 1970's was upon the preservation of the landscape beyond
the towns. Since then, however, it has been argued more forcibly that it is essential to preserve the better-quality land from development in order to ensure an
adequate food supply. The White Paper Food from our own Resources (Cmnd.6020),
which announced this strengthening of resolve by the government, was followed by
the publication of the Scottish Development Department's Planning Guidelines in
the late 1970's, which were even firmer than the White Paper in this respect. However, unlike a number of states in the U.S.A., authorities in this country do not
possess the power to encourage the use of idle farm land. In the U.S.A., where
taxes are levied on land values, some authorities grant reductions in return for a
commitment on the part of the owner to keep the land in rural use, and others seek
to compensate owners by purchasing the development rights on land close to the edge
of the built-up area. The Community Land Act 1975 in this country also was intended
to provide local authorities with powers to acquire the development rights in land
and to direct the pattern of urban development more positively than hitherto, but
with its repeal those powers have been lost. Thus the present situation in Scotland
is that, while development control and the Development Land Tax may have the effect
of reducing the hopes of owners of better-quality agricultural lands that they might
be able to sell to developers, they do not do anything to offset the extra costs
which rural users in the urban fringe suffer or to oblige such people to continue
to make use of their land in spite of these costs. On the other hand money has been
made available in increasing quantities by central government since the 1960's to
reclaim derelict land, and the Scottish Development Agency has undertaken many land
renewal projects, some of which have been at or near the edges of towns and have
returned land to agriculture and to forestry.

THE URBAN FRINGE IN SCOTLAND

What, then, is the present pattern of land use in the urban fringe in Scotland?
Have a combination of land zoning and other protective designations together with
government support of the prices of agricultural products and the absence of taxes
on land value of the American type ensured that land is only released for development at the moment when it is required, or has the land market become so imperfect
that Coleman's conclusions from England that there is a large and growing area of
idle land of high agricultural capability, and that this is concentrated around our
cities, apply also to Scotland?

In order to answer these questions the land around three urban settlements was
examined. Edinburgh was chosen because of its size and because it is surrounded
by a Green Belt which has been approved by the Secretary of State and incorporated
in the city's Development Plan. Perth was included as an example of a medium-sized
town and because it is bordered in part by "Areas of Great Landscape Value"; and
Glenrothes was selected as an example of a New Town. All are surrounded by land
of varying agricultural capability, but much is of the Macaulay Institute's Classes
2 and 3, and is considered to be prime agricultural land by the Department of
Agriculture and Fisheries for Scotland. In each case the edge of the continuously
built-up area was mapped during the spring of 1981, as were "islands" of farmland
within in. Public parks, cemeteries, golf courses and playing fields were included
within the built-up area, and where, as in the case of Holyrood Park, the land is
in both agricultural and recreational use, the latter was allowed to determine its
classification.

Several methods of measurement were applied to the unused land around these settlements. In the first place Coleman's method, in which a wide swathe of territory around the settlement is subject to a random sample of grid references, was adopted. 410 km^2 around Edinburgh was examined by the use of a random sample at 308 points. (The area covered is shown in Fig. 10.2). All land which had lain outside the built-up area of the city at the time of the Second Land Utilisation Survey, but which has subsequently been added to it, was included, together with almost all of the Green Belt. (The irregularities in the boundaries of the area which was covered were caused by the lack of a complete cover by the Second Land Utilisation Survey). The results of this random sample are shown in Tables la and lb, where it may be seen that at fourteen of the 308 points in 1981, or between four and five percent, the land was unused, and that in the Green Belt it was about two percent. These figures are less than those produced by Coleman for the Thames Estuary area in the 1970's, but similar to her total for that area when taken together with others in Merseyside and Surrey.

TABLE 10.1a Land Use Around Edinburgh 1966-1981

		Land Use in 1981					
		IMPROVED FARM LAND	WOOD	ROUGH GRAZING	BUILT-UP	UNUSED	TOTAL
Land Use according to the Second Land Utilisation Survey (1966-72)	IMPROVED FARM LAND	167	2	-	22	2	193
	WOOD	3	20	-	2	1	26
	ROUGH GRAZING	5	6	42	-	-	53
	BUILT-UP	1	-	-	16	7	24
	UNUSED	5	-	-	3	4	12
	TOTAL	181	28	42	43	14	308

TABLE 10.1b Land Use in the Edinburgh Green Belt 1966-1981

		Land Use in 1981					
		IMPROVED FARM LAND	WOOD	ROUGH GRAZING	BUILT-UP	UNUSED	TOTAL
Land Use according to the Second Land Utilisation Survey (1966-72)	IMPROVED FARM LAND	68	2	-	10	1	81
	WOOD	3	11	-	1	-	15
	ROUGH GRAZING	1	1	23	-	-	25
	BUILT-UP	-	-	-	7	1	8
	UNUSED	4	-	-	-	1	5
	TOTAL	76	14	23	18	3	134

However, these results do not tell us a great deal about the effect of Edinburgh upon the land around it. In the first place, some comparison is required with areas which do not contain urban settlements, but which have similar physical environments. Two sample areas covering 49 km^2 were selected and comprehensively surveyed for idle land. The areas were the 1:10,000 Ordnance Survey sheets No. 22 NE, which covers most of the parish of Inchture in the Carse of Gowrie, and No. 41 NW, which included

most of the parish of Dairsie in north-east Fife. It was found that 1.4 percent
of the land in those areas was unused - a lower figure than that for the environs
of Edinburgh, though not very different from that for the Green Belt. Secondly,
if the city does exert an idling effect, Fig. 10.1 suggests that it is most likely
to occur, all other things being equal, on land lying closest to the built-up area.
However, the use of Coleman-type boundaries for the area which was subject to the
random sample means that not only were they arbitrary, but also that they included
land at a great distance from the edge of the city. It would not be surprising to
learn in these circumstances that this has averaged the effect of the city over
too wide an area, and so under-estimated it. For these reasons a second measure
was employed. Unused land adjacent to the continuously built-up area was mapped,
and the results are shown in Fig. 10.3 and Table 10.2. Similar surveys were made
of Glenrothes and Perth (Figs. 10.4 and 10.5). The table shows that, in relation
to the areas of Edinburgh and Perth, the extent of the idle land was small, and it
could be concluded that the idling effect of these settlements has been weak.

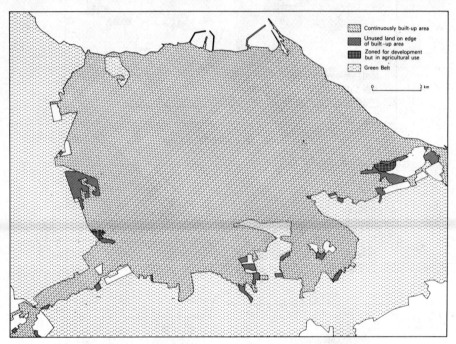

Fig. 10.3   UNUSED LAND AROUND EDINBURGH

TABLE 10.2   Unused Land on the Edge of the Continuously Built-up Area
                       as a Percentage of that Area

Edinburgh	2.4
Glenrothes	9.7
Perth	1.9

But these findings are based on aggregate figures, and closer examination of the
individual parcels of dormant land reveals considerable differences between the
different places included in the study. Most of the unused land recorded in the
random sample around Edinburgh had been used by extractive industries, or railways,
or had been built up in some other way before falling out of use. Only about a
fifth of it was last used in agriculture or forestry. In the sample areas in Fife

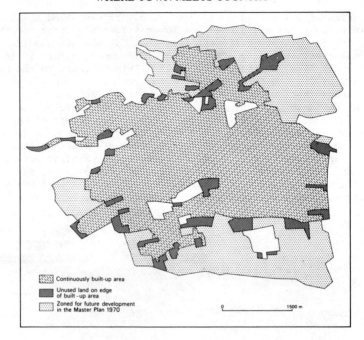

Fig. 10.4   GLENROTHES 1981

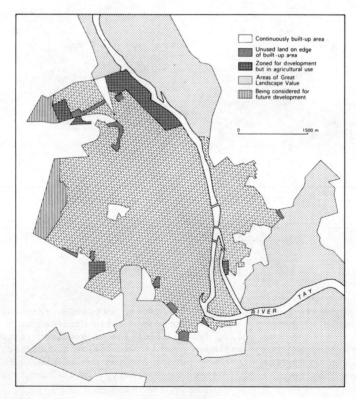

Fig. 10.5   PERTH 1981

and Perthshire, almost all of the unused land was derelict following quarrying, or
was in small parcels associated with rocky outcrops or marshy conditions which were
isolated amid prime agricultural land. On the edge of the three urban areas, in
contrast, more than three-quarters of the idle land had last been used for farming;
the parcels were larger, and much had been acquired from the previous users with a
view to future development which had not yet taken place. This is especially true
of Glenrothes, where the ratio of unused land to the built-up area is excep-
tionally high.   Further investigation is required there to establish the extent
to which this is the result of the publication in 1970 of the Master Plan which
showed that wide areas of land around the town are to be developed - a situation in
stark contrast to the modest proposals for urban expansion in the Edinburgh and
Perth Development Plans - which may have encouraged the previous users to abandon
that land, or the result of the isolation of pockets of farmland by the rapid expansion of the town, or whether the more rapid expansion of the built-up area there
than in the cases of Edinburgh or Perth necessarily requires a higher ratio of idle
to developed land. Whatever the reason, the contrast which has been revealed between
the nature of the idle land on the city edges and in the wider rural areas is crucial
to the conclusions of this study, for it shows that it is precisely at those edges
rather than in other locations that prime agricultural land is falling out of use.

However, these conclusions have been based on surveys undertaken in a single year,
and it is of some interest to know whether city-edge land has been falling out of
use to an increasing extent in the recent past, and to a greater degree than land
in other parts of the country, as Coleman has suggested in the case of the English
conurbations. Her suggestion was based upon the comparison of the results of
random point surveys in the early 1970's with the Second Land Utilisation Survey
from the previous decade, and the same method has been adopted in this study. The
results are shown in Table 10.3.   in this case the comparison was complicated by the
varying and, in some areas, unknown dates at which the Second Land Utilisation Survey
was carried out, but the overall trend is consistent and indicates that the unused
area has increased over the last ten or fifteen years in all parts of the country
under examination and not only on the edge of the cities.

TABLE 10.3   Unused Land in the Second Land Utilisation Survey
and in 1981

| | Date of 2nd L.U.S. | Unused Land | | |
		2nd L.U.S.	1981	Ratio
No 22 NE and No 41 NW[1]	1967	0.7	1.4	1:2
Edinburgh[2]	1966-72	3.9	4.5	1:1.2
Glenrothes[3]	No date	7.3	9.7	1:1.3

[1] Unused land as a percentage of all land.

[2] Unused land as a percentage of all land. The percentages were
derived from Table 1a.

[3] Unused land adjacent to the edge of the continuously built-up
area as a percentage of that area.

Furthermore, the findings show that the annual rates of increase around Glenrothes
and Edinburgh have been much less than those recorded by Coleman in the English

conurbations, and that they may well have been less than those in places away from
the cities. These findings do not suggest that the Scottish cities have been
exerting an increasingly powerful and malign influence over the farmland around
them of late. In fact, Table 10.1 shows that farmland losses to the city appear to
have been much more likely as the direct result of development, but that some of
this was recovered through the improvement and reclamation of other lands for
agriculture, both within and outside the Green Belt.

CONCLUSION

The findings of this study indicate that some land of high agricultural potential
is lying idle on the edges of Scottish cities, that the amount of idle land is
increasing, and that there is still a greater likelihood of idling in those locations than in the country as a whole. However, urban settlements cover such a
small proportion of the country that even if on average the unused area adjacent
to all of them were found to be as high as that around Glenrothes, less than one
percent of the country's agricultural and forest land would be lying dormant as a
direct result of urban influences. Moreover, insofar as the study has concentrated
on settlements in the most fertile areas of Scotland it is unlikely that, even if
higher rates of idling exist elsewhere, they will significantly upset the general
conclusion that idling presents no serious challenge to the government's effort
to protect the agricultural potential of the country. In short, neither the
suggestion that a massive misuse of land is occurring at the point where the city
meets the country, nor the conclusion that the powers of the authorities should
be extended still further to combat such misuse, can be sustained.

REFERENCES

Berry, D., 1976. Idling of Farmland in the Philadelphia Region 1930-1970. Regional
    Science Research Institute Discussion Paper Series 88.
Coleman, A., 1978. Agricultural land losses: the evidence from maps. In Urban
    Growth, Farmland Losses and Planning, ed. A.W. Rogers, pp. 16-36, Wye College,
    London.
Coppock, J.T., 1978. Discussion. In Urban Growth, Farmland Losses and Planning,
    ed. A.W. Rogers, pp. 37-58, Wye College, London.
Coughlin, R.E., Berry, D. and Bieri, K. 1977. Saving the Garden: The Preservation
    of Farmland and Other Environmentallt Valuable Land. Regional Science Research
    Institute, Philadelphia.
Coughlin, R.E. 1979. Agricultural Land Conversion in the Urban-Rural Fringe,
    Regional Science Research Institute Discussion Paper Series III.
Glenrothes Development Corporation, 1970. Glenrothes New Town Master Plan Report
    1970, Glenrothes
Leeming, F. and Sousson, J., 1979. Structures at the fringe of the city.
    International Social Science Journal 31, pp. 273-281.
Low, N., 1973. Farming and the Inner Green Belt. Town Planning Review, 44, pp. 103-
    116.
Ministry of Agriculture, Fisheries and Food 1975. Food from our own Resources
    (Cmnd. 6020). H.M.S.O., London.
Munton, R.J., 1974. Farming on the Urban Fringe. In Suburban Growth, ed. J.H.
    Johnson, pp. 201-223, Wiley, London.
Scottish Development Department 1977. Planning Guidelines, Edinburgh.
Smith, J.S. 1980. Agricultural land use consequent on development in the Moray
    Firth sub-region with comparative data from the Grampian Region. Moray Firth
    Development Ecological Study, Interim Report No. 10, University of Aberdeen.
U.S. Department of Commerce 1979. Preserving America's Farmland - A Goal the
    Federal Government should support, Springfield.

CHAPTER 11

PLANNING POLICY IN THE CLYDE VALLEY GREEN BELT

Alan W. Aitken
Strathclyde Regional Council

ABSTRACT

The object of this paper is to examine the use of Green Belt policy as a means of controlling development in the western part of the Clyde Valley Green Belt. This will be approached through an analysis of the types of development applications that arise in the Green Belt and the manner in which they are handled by the local planning authorities

KEYWORDS

Clyde Valley Regional Plan; Green Belt; development control records; Regional Council; District Council.

THE CLYDE VALLEY GREEN BELT

The Clyde Valley Regional Plan of 1946 (Abercrombie and Matthew, 1949) proposed the Green Belt in order to restrict the suburban growth of Glasgow and as a corollary to the central principle to the Plan, namely the decentralisation of population from Glasgow where housing densities were extremely high. The Green Belt designation would protect the good quality agricultural land around the Conurbation and a series of New Towns would be developed to receive the people displaced from Glasgow. The result of these two measures was "... a polynucleated urban system designed on a very tight pattern and set in a green background" (Grieve, 1945, p.16).

During the 1950s the concept of the Green Belt received the support of Central Government with the publication of Circular No. 42/1955 which gave the main purposes for the designation of a Green Belt as:

1) to check the further growth of a large built-up area:

2) to prevent neighbouring towns from coalescing; and

3) to preserve the special character of a town.

(M.H.L.G., 1962).

Although this Circular applied only to England and Wales, the Scottish Office issued

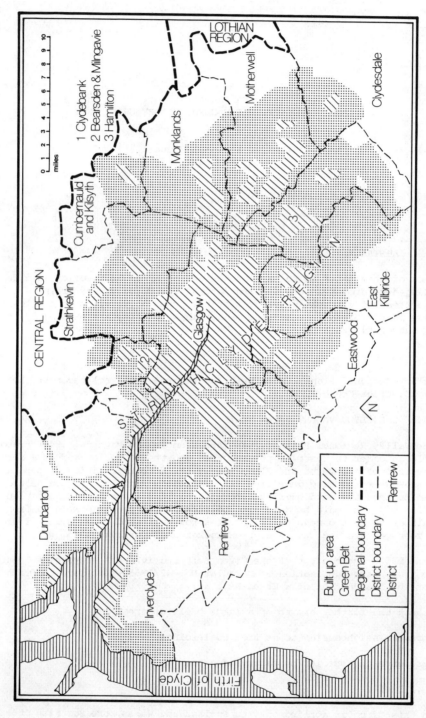

Fig. 11.1   THE CLYDE VALLEY GREEN BELT

similar advice in Circular No. 40/1960, and the County Councils in the Clyde Valley Region incorporated the main points of the Circular into their Development Plans and development control policies. The aims of the decentralisation of population from Glasgow and the protection of the agricultural land around the Conurbation which had been emphasised in the Clyde Valley Regional Plan, had become rather obscured in the County Development Plans.

In 1953 Lanark County Council had submitted their Central Industrial Area Plan containing Green Belt proposals to the Secretary of State. This plan was approved in 1958, and after the Circular of 1960 the Development Plans for Renfrewshire (1964), Dunbartonshire Western Area (1964) and Lanark Northern and Southern Areas (1965) were approved. The Large Burghs which were the other local planning authorities at that time were not in favour of the Green Belt because of their need for housing land within their boundaries due to inner city redevelopment. As a result the Large Burghs did not designate any Green Belt on their Town Maps.

Fig. 11.1 shows that following the re-organisation of local government into a two-tier system of Regions and Districts in 1975, the Clyde Valley Green Belt fell almost entirely within the Strathclyde Region, and the responsibility of planning in the Green Belt was shared by Strathclyde Regional Council and fourteen District Councils. At the same time, a two-tier development plan system of Structure Plans and Local Plans, was also introduced.

In the Strathclyde Structure Plan Written Statement in 1979 the Regional Council set down the following policy for the Green Belt:

"The spread of built up areas and the encroachment of development into the country-side within a 'Greenbelt' around the Conurbation ..... shall not accord with the Regional Development Strategy." (S.R.C. 1979, p. 58).

By thus restricting development in the Green Belt this policy complements the main aim of the Regional Strategy which is to encourage the redevelopment of the older declining parts of the Conurbation by directing residential or industrial develop-ment there in preference to Green Belt locations.

The District Councils for their part seem to favour restrictive Green Belt policies similar to those implemented by the former County Councils but it will be interest-ing to see how these authorities which contain urban and rural areas cope with the problems of urban expansion at the same time as protecting the countryside around the towns.

The analysis described below tried to establish the extent to which the actions of the local planning authorities implemented the policies that they put forward for the Green Belt in their development plans during this period of change.

        THE CONTEXT OF THE STUDY

The area selected for this study was the District of Renfrew lying to the west of Glasgow, for an extensive area of the Green Belt designated by the former Renfrew County Council in the County Development Plan lies within Renfrew District. It is the intention of the District Council to continue to operate the policies of the County Council in these Green Belt areas until they have produced a Local Plan for the rural area which will include Green Belt policies. This plan is expected to be approved in 1982.

By analysing the development control records of the County Council and the District Council it was possible to build up a picture of the types of development application that were likely to arise in the Green Belt. During the period 1970-78 almost five hundred applications were received in the study area and of these 195 occurred in 1973, 1975 and 1977. By selecting these years it was hoped that any changes in policy through time might become evident. In his study of the West Midlands Green Belt, Gregory (1970) emphasised the importance of studying develop- ment control records over several years in order to understand the decision making process and to evaluate the cumulative results on the ground, for it is by this that the public will judge the success of Green Belt policy.

The existence of a Green Belt on an approved development plan can act as a deterrent to potential applicants who are advised by the planning department about the possibility of refusal on Green Belt grounds so that the actual number of applicat- ions received represents only a proportion of those that might have been made.

"A green belt in its restrictive sense can only be sensibly adopted in close conjunction with other planning measures." (Self in Long, ed., 1961, p.XV).

The other measures referred to here include the allocation of land for residential purposes in recognition of the demand for private housing. Renfrew County Council planned to create new communities at Erskine and Houston to accommodate this demand and amended the Development Plan accordingly.

Tables 1 and 2 show the range of applications received by the District Council during the selected years. In analysing the development control decisions, which represent the principal means of implementing local authority planning policy, it is important to remember that every application is judged on its merits. Neverthe- less, in terms of the policy formulated for the Green Belt, recreational, tipping and dumping, public utilities, agricultural and miscellaneous applications fall within conforming uses of Green Belt land. Residential, storage, industrial and commercial uses would normally be non-conforming uses except where residence related to agriculture and industry to mineral working.

TABLE 11.1   Development Control in Renfrew District 1973
and 1 January - 15 May 1975

Category	Approved	Refused	Other
1. RESIDENTIAL:			
Private development	3	9	1
Single house	20	11	1
Alterations/extensions	19	2	1
Rehabilitation	–	1	–
Change of use (to house)	1	–	–
Residential caravan	8	2	–
Caravan site	–	1	–
2. RECREATION	5	–	2
3. TIPPING/DUMPING	7	1	–
4. STORAGE	7	4	–
5. COMMERCIAL	3	1	–
6. INDUSTRIAL	3	6	–
7. PUBLIC UTILITIES	5	–	–
8. AGRICULTURAL	5	1	–
9. MISCELLANEOUS			
Roads and car parks	3	–	–
Religious	1	–	–
Totals	90	39	5

TABLE 11.2   Development Control in Renfrew District
15 May - 31 December 1975 and 1977

Category	Approved	Refused	Other
1. RESIDENTIAL:			
Private development	1	5	-
Single house	5	11	1
Alterations/extensions	9	2	2
Rehabiliation	-	1	-
Residential caravan	1	-	-
2. RECREATION	2	-	-
3. TIPPING/DUMPING	4	-	1
4. STORAGE	2	2	-
5. COMMERCIAL	1	2	-
6. INDUSTRIAL	2	-	-
7. PUBLIC UTILITIES	2	-	-
8. AGRICULTURAL	1	-	-
9. MISCELLANEOUS			
Roads and car parks	1	2	-
Reservoir	-	-	1
Totals	31	25	5

Fig. 11.2 shows the extent of the Green Belt in Renfrew District and the locations of the applications on a kilometre grid basis.

RESIDENTIAL DEVELOPMENT CONTROL

Tables 11.1 and 11.2 show that for the three years under study the greatest number of applications for development in the Green Belt relate to some form of residential development. The size of these proposals varies from the erection of front and rear dormer windows on a single house to the development of up to twenty hectares of farmland for private housing. In terms of area it is private housing development for two or more houses which puts the greatest pressure on the Green Belt.

Of the nineteen applications for this type of development only four were approved and all of these refer to the same site on the southern edge of Neilston, for after outline permission had been given several detailed applications were submitted and approved by the County (1973) and District (1975) Councils.

Fourteen applications for private housing development were refused. Among these were two applications by a private landowner to develop eight hectares adjoining the village of Kilbarchan for housing. Renfrew County Council refused these applications for the following reasons:

1) the land was zoned for agriculture;

2) the land was in the Green Belt;

3) development there would harm amenity;

4) it would create an undesirable precedent;

5)   there were problems of drainage in the area;

6)   there was a lack of education facilities in the village.

This example is typical of the response to applications for private housing development in the Green Belt and it shows how infrastructure constraints can be used to
support the restrictive nature of Green Belt policy.

When a development application is refused by the local planning authority, the
applicant can appeal to the Secretary of State against this decision.   The records
of Renfrew County Council revealed one of these cases relating to the development
of 20 hectares of land for private housing to the north of Bishopton.   Although
the town had been expanding rapidly in the 1960s, Renfrew County Council refused
the application in 1974, probably because there was adequate land zoned for housing
at Erskine and Houston, and the Secretary of State upheld this decision in 1976.

The largest group of applications in the residential category is for single houses.
In addition to the forty-nine for new houses there were three applications for the
change of use of farm buildings to houses or for the re-building of semi-derelict
property for housing.   Altogether twenty-six of these applications were approved.
An important factor in these cases is whether the house will be used by an
agricultural worker or not, for agriculture is one of the approved uses of Green
Belt land, but even where this was the case the planning authority still refused
three of these applications.

The other large group of residential applications consisted of alterations and
extensions to existing houses.   These small scale changes made little impact on
the Green Belt in overall terms but because they are almost all approved, they
tend to make Green Belt policy seem less effective as a means of development
control.

Seven of the applications for residential caravans were for agricultural workers
and although all except one were approved, they were only given temporary permission for one to three years.   Single residential caravans take up very little area,
but sporadic development of this sort would be as harmful to the amenity of the
Green Belt as sporadic housing.   By issuing only temporary approvals the District
Council is able to keep a regular check on the number and location of these
developments.

NON-RESIDENTIAL DEVELOPMENT CONTROL

Applications for recreation and leisure developments seem to have had complete
support from the District and County Councils.   Two of these applications were
related to the establishment of a nature centre and associated facilities by the
Royal Society for the Protection of Birds near Lochwinnoch.   The development of a
golf course connected with a private recreation club, the opening of wooded grounds
to the public and the creation of two football pitches with a clubhouse were among
the other applications in this category approved by the Local Planning Authorities.

The Green Belt is subject to pressure for the development of public utilities such
as sewage works and refuse incineration plants and the applicants for these are
usually the Regional or District Councils.   All of the applications for this type
of development in Renfrew District were approved.   However, there was one case
where agreement between the Local Authorities had not been reached.   This concerned
the draining of a reservoir near Howwood by Strathclyde Regional Council with the
intention of using the resulting land for agriculture or recreation.   Local fishing
interests opposed the plan and the District Council made no decision on it.

Agriculture is considered to be the principal land use of the Green Belt but as it is largely outside planning control, very few applications were received for developments related to agriculture in the study period. All six applications for agricultural buildings which included a poultry processing and packing factory and a poultry laying house, were approved.

Closely connected with agricultural land use is the varied collection of applications grouped under the heading of tipping and dumping in Tables 11.1 and 11.2. The majority of these were approved including the infilling of old quarries with refuse and the removal of subsoil and rock to be used in adjacent motorway construction on the M8 near Bishopton, again emphasising the use of the Green Belt as a service corridor.

Finally, there are the industrial, commercial and storage applications. Although such developments would appear to be contrary to Green Belt policy about half of hem were approved. However, very few of these represented new development as most were related to established uses. Old farm buildings are sometimes used for light industrial purposes or for caravan storage and several applications of this sort were received in Renfrew District. One of the largest industrial applications was for the development of maturation warehouses on eighteen hectares of agricultural land near Inchinnan but this was refused on Green Belt grounds and because there was sufficient land zoned for industry elsewhere in the County.

CONCLUSION

The data presented in Tables 1 and 2 show that the ratio of approvals to refusals fell from 2:1 in the period before Local Government re-organisation to almost 1:1 after re-organisation. The most significant feature of this change is the higher rate of refusals for single houses which seems to indicate that the District Council is operating a more stringent policy towards sporadic residential development than the County Council did and the Green Belt is a key instrument in this policy.

By limiting housing and industry to specially zoned land, it has been possible for the local authorities to prevent massive urban intrusions into the Green Belt during the study period. By this means, they have prevented neighbouring towns and villages from merging and preserved the special historic character of villages such as Kilbarchan.

The results of this study confirm the overall impression of the Green Belt as a means of restriction and containment upheld by both Regional and District Councils despite the changing economic and social conditions which have created much vacant land in the urban areas and have reduced the pressure to build in the Green Belt.

REFERENCES

Abercrombie, P. and Matthew, R.H. 1949. The Clyde Valley Regional Plan. 1946. H.M.S.O., Edinburgh.

Gregory, D. 1970. Green Belts and Development Control. Centre for Urban and Regional Studies, University of Birmingham, Birmingham.

Grieve, R. 1954. The Clyde Valley - a Review. Town and Country Planning Summer School.

Long, J.R. (Ed.) 1961. The Wythall Inquiry. Estates Gazette, London.

Ministry of Housing and Local Government 1962. The Green Belts. H.M.S.O., London.

Strathclyde Regional Council, 1979. Strathclyde Structure Plan Written Statement, Glasgow.

Dunbarton County Council, 1961. Western Area Part Development Plan Written
    Statement. Dumbarton.
Lanark County Council, 1953. Central Industrial Area Development Plan Written
    Statement, Hamilton.
Lanark County Council, 1962. Lanark Northern and Southern Areas Development Plan
    Written Statement, Hamilton.
Renfrew County Council, 1962. County Development Plan Written Statement. Paisley.

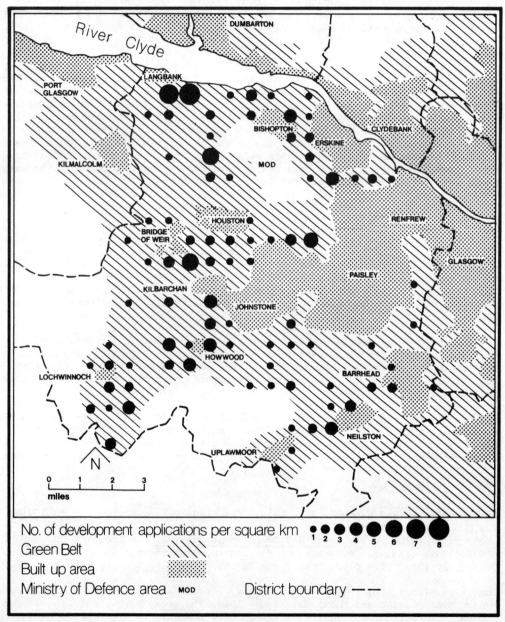

Fig. 11.2 DEVELOPMENT APPLICATIONS IN RENFREW DISTRICT GREEN BELT IN 1973, 1975
AND 1977

CHAPTER 12
MANAGING THE LAND SUPPLY

Roger Pead
Strathclyde Regional Council

ABSTRACT

Strathclyde Region is used as an example to demonstrate the problems faced by
Regional Authorities in Scotland in managing the land supply for development. The
Structure Plan is the medium it uses to do this. The author emphasises the need
for flexibility and frequent review of the development land demand/supply situation
and of the availability of sites as a result of urban renewal as against the use
of greenfield sites on the urban fringe.

KEYWORDS

The Housing Supply; Brownfield and Greenfield and Housing Demand; The Industrial
Land Supply; Large Sites and Vacant Land; Industrial Demand; Urban Renewal;
The Urban Fringe.

One of the things that only a Regional Council can do is to manage the Development Land Supply. This is difficult enough when a Conurbation is prospering and
expanding, but it is doubly difficult in a period of decline. A delicate balance
has to be struck between the re-use of urban land, what might be called "brownfield" development, and the use of the surrounding countryside for what might be
called "greenfield" development. This paper outlines Strathclyde's approach to
the problem in its Structure Plan.

When Local Government was re-organised in 1975, it proved quite difficult simply to
assemble a factual picture of the real land supply. Only slowly has it been
established which sites have existing planning consent where future development
has to be accepted whether it is well located or not, and the vacant urban land,
to which future development has to be attracted, been identified. The trick is to
balance what can reasonably be expected by way of development from these two
sources with the need to release any more greenfield land.

The Strathclyde Structure Plan, approved by the Secretary of State this January,
establishes that no further greenfield release is required until the middle of
1982. After that the situation is fraught with uncertainty and the question is
how to cope with it.

115

THE HOUSING LAND SUPPLY, BROWNFIELD AND GREENFIELD AND HOUSING DEMAND

Prediction is not what is required in such a situation. It is more a question of
establishing the range of probability and considering how to cope with the consequences at either extreme. For example, private housebuilding has been running at
a rate of between 4,000 and 5,000 houses a year in the Region. The housebuilders
feel it could rise to 6,000, 7,000 or even 8,000 a year in the eighties, yet there
are factors which could have the reverse effect. Given the lead-in time to bring
land to the point of development, a five year land supply is the minimum required.
A few simple sums and it can be seen that the land needed could vary between 1,000
and 2,000 hectares for 20,000 to 40,000 houses.

Against this there is a substantial amount of land with planning consent. It has
capacity for 25,000 to 30,000 houses but much of this is on large sites which, if
developed in a viable way, would not be completed in five years, so it has to be
accepted that only about 80% of the consents are really available. Likewise there
is a massive amount of uncommitted vacant urban land, something like 2200 hectares
within the Region, but only a small proportion, probably no more than 100 to 300
hectares with a capacity of between 2,500 and 7,500 houses, could be seriously
considered for housing development in the next five years.

Looking beyond the mid-1980s therefore, the land supply could conceivably need to
be supplemented by substantial new greenfield housing sites. On the other hand it
could prove sufficient to last into the 1990s if the market turns out to be low.

In Strathclyde Region, over 60% of housing is in the public sector and private
housing tends to be concentrated in a few well established areas such as Eastwood,
Bearsden and Milngavie and Strathkelvin. Much of the impetus for further private
housing is bound to come from the public sector and there would seem to be a good
case for seeking a better balance of new private housebuilding between traditional
areas and the post-war council housing around the periphery. Unfortunately, this
is easier said than done because areas in the eastern Conurbation suffer particularly from undermining and a lack of services such as sewers and water supplies,
and of course the Conurbation is surrounded by high quality agricultural land.

Somehow all these matters have to be brought to a sensible conclusion. When the
District Councils were asked to identify land which, from a local planning point of
view, might be considered for release, it turned out to have a capacity for as much
as 70,000 houses. Only land for 7,700 houses could be developed without major infrastructure provision, and of this only 5,500 houses could be developed on non prime
agricultural land.

Even then, much of t his is in traditional areas and its development would only
reinforce the established imbalances. However, there are locations in the north
east of Glasgow and between Monklands and Motherwell where housing development
would be advantageous in many ways, where conflict with agricultural land could be
minimised, but which unfortunately would be costly to develop.

The issue for the Council has therefore turned out to be reasonably straightforward.
To what extent can land in beneficial locations be brought forward at some cost, to
minimise the land which may otherwise have to be released in less beneficial areas
but at little cost? This is one of the issues which is currently up for discussion
in the first Review of the Structure Plan. If beneficial land is released and it
turns out to be more than was needed then the worst that may happen is that greenfield sites in traditional areas will have some competition. It has also been
argued that development on vacant urban land would be prejudiced, and it will
certainly be necessary to sustain a balance. However, inner area sites should be

able to stand on their own merits, if they are marketed on the right terms.

In order to strike and maintain a balance between the fluctuating demand for private housing and the various sources of supply of land, Strathclyde has considered a "review/reserve" approach whereby the Structure Plan is reviewed and rolled forward every two years, and a reserve of land is identified and safeguarded for release as required. For example, there would appear to be a case for the further release of land between 1982 and 1987 for an additional 6 - 7,000 houses in the Clyde Valley area over and above the existing land supply. This would allow an average building rate of about 5,000 houses over the period. However, if the housebuilders are proved right and rates of 6,000 or 7,000 are achieved, then a reserve land supply has been identified which could be brought forward when the Plan is next reviewed by 1984. In this way the contingency of a high rate of development is planned for but no premature commitment needs to be made by way of pipes in the ground or schools in the locality. At a time of constrained public expenditure a cautious approach is unavoidable.

The question of private housing has been dealt with because it is by far the most probable source of future pressure on the urban fringe. There is evidence of greater housing availability in the public sector, where future demand is likely to be for special needs such as sheltered housing on sites within existing housing, and for the modernisation of the existing stock, rather than for greenfield development. The exception could be the New Towns, but at East Kilbride the housing position will become similar to the more attractive parts of the Conurbation, which have now reached real environmental constraints affecting their setting or conflicting head on with agricultural interests.

There is, however, a practical problem associated with the review/release approach and that is how reserve land is to be treated in Local Plans. Clearly planning consents should not be given on reserve land until the Structure Plan indicates the need to do so. If development is slow then reserve land could remain under some blight. Here there is a clear balance of risk to be weighed up. On the one hand, the prospect of a housing land shortage could inflate land values, whereas, on the other hand, over zoning could generate blight. A prospective shortage means that developers feel obliged to increase the supply through planning applications and appeals on an ad hoc basis, whereas a generous supply at least means that the planning system can make a more objective choice of land, weighing up all, sometimes, conflicting interests such as cost, agricultural or housing need. It means also that the provision of support services such as schools, roads and pipes can be planned and budgeted for on a more considered basis rather than in response to unforeseen circumstances. Local plans too have some view of possibilities beyond 5 years and of the probable need or otherwise for continuity of development. It does mean, however, that the planning system has to stay on its toes and keep plans up to date and flexible. At the moment the system is sadly lacking in this respect, and the burden of the statutory processes does not help.

THE INDUSTRIAL LAND SUPPLY, LARGE SITES AND VACANT LAND, AND INDUSTRIAL DEMAND

The other main areas for development around the urban fringe are the larger industrial sites. It is becoming quite clear now that the case for reserving 40 to 100 hectare sites for prospective single users is not too strong. The Region has 8 recognised sites in this category and some 20-25 sites in the 10 to 30 hectare category where prospects may be better. These larger sites represent the Region's shop window for inward investment of the more spectacular kind. It needs to be recognised however, that there have been only some 2 or 3 developments in the over 100 hectare category annually in the whole of western Europe over the last 10

years, none of which have been in Scotland. Indeed there have only been 9 Scottish
developments in the 10-30 hectare range.

Out of a total supply of 1,000 hectares of readily developable industrial land in
the Region only about 60 hectares are taken up annually, and by far the greater
part of this is for advance factories on SDA or New Town estates. It can be
concluded that prospects for industrial development are very limited in relation
to the total available land supply and that two main sources of demand will probably
remain. Firstly, in the under 2.5 hectare category for small scale workshops and
advance factories on a speculative basis by the public sector, and secondly in the
medium size 10-30 hectare category for specific incoming or expanding plants by the
private sector. As a generalisation the smaller developments are readily accommodated on brownfield sites, and the opportunities for larger developments lie on
the periphery in greenfield or urban fringe locations, such as Inchinnan, Darnley,
Cambuslang and Newhouse.

This gives rise to two problems. On the one hand, there is bound to be a substantial
amount of vacant urban land with no immediate prospects of housing or industrial
development, which will remain unused and uncared for. There are indications that
the SDA's land renewal funds will be directed in future to the recovery of urban
land which has some hope of industrial or commercial development. Thus there will
be a real need for some cheap and relatively mainteance free treatment of vacant
land. On the other hand, large industrial sites will remain in the urban fringe
with only limited prospects of use, and a consequent degree of blight.

THE GREENBELT

The Structure Plan makes provision for an extensive greenbelt around the Conurbation
with the expressed intent of preventing urban sprawl and coalescence and protecting
the countryside. The aim is to keep the countryside productive as far as possible
right up to the urban edge. Around most of the Conurbation the urban edge is
relatively distinct with something of a clear-cut boundary between town and country.
In the broad area bounded by Rutherglen, Motherwell, Coatbridge, Airdrie and Easterhouse however, all the urban fringe problems can be seen. Agricultural land,
although of good quality, is fragmented and under pressure. There is a legacy of
dereliction from the extractive and heavy industries and the landscape is blighted.
It has many of the unfortunate characteristics of the twilight fringe which is
neither urban nor rural in character, and the Structure Plan has identified it as
the place most in need of improved use and management. Hopefully, the Countryside
Commission will share this view and rise to the challenge to support the local
authorities with funds and expertise.

The area falls into two distinct parts. Firstly around Newton the Clyde itself
presents an opportunity to link Strathclyde Park to the city with a riverside park,
and steps have been taken in this direction. The Hallside works could provide land
for housing but the major problem is land renewal. At Newton the emphasis could
be on a range of small scale initiatives to manage the land to better agricultural
or recreational effect. Secondly at Chapelhall between Monklands and Motherwell
there lies the North Calder Valley which again has recreational potential, but more
importantly there is the Newhouse industrial site of about 90 hectares. 25 hectares
are to be reserved for any large single development of national significance, but
there is additional scope for sites in the 10-30 hectare range. At Chapelhall and
beyond Easterhouse the Structure Plan has identified two major areas of search for
new private housing with a joint capacity of 6,500 dwellings. At Chapelhall the
emphasis could be on housing and industrial development of some significance.

URBAN RENEWAL AND THE URBAN FRINGE

To sum up then, the Regional picture is one of limited development prospects, but of substantial opportunities particularly within the eastern portion of the Conurbation. It is here that development can be allied to land management and land renewal to achieve the recovery and more effective use of the urban fringe. It is here that such related action would also bring social and economic benefits to a sector of the Conurbation which is at a disadvantage.

So although Strathclyde's strategy is essentially one of urban renewal this is not inconsistent with a need for greenfield development where this has associated benefits to adjoining urban areas and the urban fringe.

COMMENT ON CHAPTERS 10, 11 and 12 BY SYMPOSIUM DISCUSSANT

Brian K. Parnell
Glasgow School of Art

The three papers by Messrs. Dawson, Aitken and Pead might well lead us to the superficial conclusion that very little is wrong with the way we are managing the countryside around towns. It would appear that green belt planning controls are effective, that local authorities under the new planning procedures are adopting the right policies to keep them effective and that the urban shadow has had little impact on our countryside. It is true, of course, that Andrew Dawson's paper dealt only with towns in the east of Scotland and he would have found higher percentages of disused land if he had come to the Clyde conurbation. Even apart from this, however, such a conclusion would be misleading if only because other land near disused land may be badly or inefficiently used and itself approaching disuse and because the pressures on the urban fringe can only grow.

The time has come for us to question the basic assumptions upon which current green belt policies are based - the policies that is which guide planners in the decisions they make on land use in the urban fringe. Essentially these are based on the concept of the green belt and the guidance given by central government on the form planning control should take within the green belt. In Scotland the best known of government circulars relevant to this is DHS Circular 40 of 1960. The green belt concept (and, of course, the DHS Circular) was adopted in a state of society very different from that in which we live today. Green belt thinking found its first expression in the London Green Belt Act 1938 which declared the objectives of the green belt as the preservation of rural character but the establishment of rec- reation as the primary land use. Abercromby's plan for the County of London in 1943 adopted these objectives and added to them the assertion that public owner- ship was necessary within the green belt which he saw as part of a park system for London.

It was the same Abercromby who three years later recommended a green belt for Glasgow in his Clyde Valley Regional Plan but for this green belt he defined different objectives. In contrast with London, Glasgow's hinterland provided plenty of opportunities for recreation beyond the watershed around the city and the land within that watershed seemed at the time to be essential for market garden produce and dairy produce for the city. Abercromby defined his green belt objec- tives as the containment of the city and the continuation of agricultural use within the green belt. All subsequently defined green belts in Scotland tended to have similarly preservationist objectives and these were broadly endorsed and strength- ened by the terms of the Department of Health Circular 40 of '60. In fact this

Circular included suggestions that environmental enhancement would be part of a
local authority's responsibility in the green belt but it has generally been used
in support of local authority policies to refuse all development in a green belt
which was not concerned directly with agricultural or forestry or which was related
to countryside recreation. Indeed the constructive parts of the Circular seem to
have been largely disregarded and it has been used as a substitute for planning
thought in the practise of development control.

Nevertheless there have been major intrusions into the green belts in Scotland but
these have not led to any reconsideration of the basic policies. Today the situation is changed in several important respects compared with the immediate pre-war
and post-war years. The need to preserve Glasgow's market garden and dairy farmland has no longer the same weight: the marketing of vegetables and dairy produce
is no longer limited to daily delivery distances. During the past 30/40 years
there has been a great increase in the demand for countryside recreation. The
problems of access and parking in city centres has led to some office decentralisation and urban pollution has made necessary the siting of some industries out
of the towns. There has also been some growth of recreation within the green belts
but many of the measures which have emerged from the countryside Acts of the late
sixties have tended to be geared to the needs of the private motorist and they are
at a distance which is inconvenient for the city dwellers without cars. The developments consequent on these pressures have been random because many of them have
entered the green belt against the wishes of the planning authority and not in
accordance, therefore, with any landscape plan for the area. At the same time the
growth of peripheral housing estates has increased the blight on peripheral agricultural land. Clearly the green belt policies are not adequate to deal with this
situation and it is time for us to review them. Our first step should be to drop
the term "green belt" altogether and to deal with the urban fringe as part of a
continuum. Today's needs are more for a garden around a town than for an agricultural zone. The garden around a house may include its vegetable patch, its garage
and garden shed but it also includes space for play and quiet recreation and a
green and attractive setting for the house. The needs for a town are the same.

Within the urban fringe the prevailing negative policies of the green belt should
be replaced by positive policies for the urban fringe. What impact would such
policies have on the planning authority and what would be their main features?
Certainly they would no longer reject all development not concerned with the productive use of the land. Local authorities might, for example, accept institutions,
offices and some types of industries where, with appropriate planning conditions
or by the use of Section 50 agreements, these would provide funds for the development
of parkland to contribute to the setting of the town and where public access might
also be secured. This kind of "planning gain" is becoming an increasingly important
feature of development control in towns and in the countryside and it can ensure
that uses which might at first seem inconsistent with the green belt could be made
to contribute positively to its character.

More country parks (of new types to suit the needs of the part of the city population which does not own cars) might be developed at locations where they could
be reached by walking or by the city's public transport system.

Where high quality parkland already exists around large country houses some new
private housing might be permitted where it would help the maintenance of the
character of the estate which today may have become too expensive for a single
owner. Project officers with funds for minor works in the countryside could be
appointed to make contact with the owners of urban fringe land and to help reconcile
the existing land uses with controlled public access.

It is not necessary to wait for major social studies to be conducted to determine

what types of recreation are appropriate in the urban fringe. What is necessary
is an experimental approach: the provision of facilities in flexible forms and
the continual monitoring of their effectiveness with a willingness to change
wherever experience makes this desirable. Indeed countryside planning for recreation is not capable of being based on firm predictions of need. It is always
an experimental science. There has, nevertheless, been a great lack of monitoring
by planning authorities and it is the discussant's view that where government money
is given as grants to local authorities for countryside recreation provisions it
should be given with a condition that whatever facility is provided should be
monitored continuously.

All these policies for the green belt must mean a loss of land from agriculture
but there would be bonuses in more land being devoted to forestry, better protection for land that remained in agriculture and some ecological gain by the creation
of new diverse habitats.

When local government was re-organised in Scotland 6 years ago towns were linked
with their hinterlands for the first time and a comprehensive approach to the
planning of the countryside around towns is therefore possible now in a way it had
not been in the past.

Many regretted that the Strathclyde Structure Plan did not include policies on
countryside recreation and tourism. At the end of his talk Mr. Pead made a statement which is very significant and hopeful. He said (in relation to part of the
urban conurbation), "It is here that development can be allied to land management
and land renewal to achieve the recovery and more effective use of the urban fringe".
This is a very brief summary of the kind of new policies which should be adopted
and it is to be hoped that a positive and comprehensive approach will soon become
part of every relevant Structure and Local Plan in Scotland.

INDEX

Only the first citation in any one chapter is given.